Introduction

So here we are, well into the new millennium and there is still no robotic classroom assistant who grades all the papers and makes sure that no one in the back of the room is talking; still no time-travel phone booth that allows us to take our class on a trip to Independence Hall, circa 1776, and still no brain-scanning technology that instantly assesses the reading-comprehension skills of our students.

Here are the facts: Contemporary educators assess students basically the same ways they were assessed fifty years ago—students read a passage and then they answer a question like this:

---

1. Why do you think the author is using humor to introduce the topic of test-taking to her audience?

    A. The author is trying to trick the reader into thinking this is a joke book.

    B. The author does not think test-taking is very important.

    C. The author has invented a brain-scanning device.

    D. The author is trying to use humor to introduce a stressful topic.

The answer is D. Standardized testing, whether you are the test-giver or the test-taker, is a high-stakes, stressful proposition, and for the time being, there's no getting away from all those tiny bubbles! So let's breathe deeply and try to figure out the most effective ways in which to help our students fill in all those tiny bubbles correctly!

Much has been written about test-taking strategies, most of it focused on the actual techniques that students can use to help navigate multiple-choice questions. While we acknowledge the necessity of that skill set, the focus of the books in this series is somewhat different.

This book concentrates on the requisite reading-comprehension skills that are prevalent on standardized multiple-choice tests and the ways in which we can teach students to first recognize the type of questions they are being asked, and second, to use the most effective strategies to answer specific types of reading-comprehension questions.

We believe that if students have an awareness, a kind of metacognition, about the specific skills that are evaluated and an ability to discriminate among the array of questions they are being asked, then they will become more confident and effective test-takers.

Explicit and Implicit Questions

Reading-comprehension tests primarily ask two types of overarching questions. These questions are either *explicit* or *implicit*.

Explicit Questions

Explicit questions are questions for which there is a literal, easy-to-find answer. These kinds of questions are also called "right there" questions because students can find the answer stated overtly right there in the text.

- Explicit questions often begin with the words *who*, *what*, *when*, or *where*.

- Explicit questions fall under the Bloom's Taxonomy category of *Remembering* (also known as *Knowledge*), requiring students to simply recall or locate information.

- Explicit questions are often the easiest reading-comprehension questions for students to answer.

Remember, to answer an explicit question, look for the answer written *right there* in the text. Locate it and point right to it!

Implicit Questions

Implicit questions are questions that require the reader to read *between the lines* to identify information that is often not stated literally but is implied by the text.

- Implicit questions require students to draw conclusions and to make deductions and predictions.

- Implicit questions frequently require that students make text-to-self and text-to-world connections.

- Implicit questions fall under the Bloom's Taxonomy category of *Analyzing and Evaluating*, which requires students to make judgments, compare and contrast, and distinguish between facts and opinions.

- Implicit questions are often extremely challenging for students to answer.

To answer an implicit question, use clues from the story plus your own experience. Implicit questions often begin with the word *why*.

Making Inferences and Drawing Conclusions

Drawing a conclusion based on implied information in a text is a skill that requires practice. In order to draw a reasonable conclusion and answer an inferential question, the reader must identify the unstated or implied information in a text, and then combine it with his or her own experiences and knowledge of the world (prior knowledge).

Use the "Boy in the Pond" activity on pages 7–9 to help students discriminate between implicit and explicit questions.

Managing Editor
Mara Ellen Guckian

Editor in Chief
Karen J. Goldfluss, M.S. Ed.

Creative Director
Sarah M. Smith

Illustrator
Clint McKnight

Cover Artist
Barb Lorseyedi

Art Coordinator
Renée Mc Elwee

Imaging
James Edward Grace
Craig Gunnell

Publisher
Mary D. Smith, M.S. Ed.

Author
Julia McMeans, M.Ed.

For correlations to the Common Core State Standards, see pages 10–11. Correlations can also be found at *http://www.teachercreated.com/standards.*

Teacher Created Resources
6421 Industry Way
Westminster, CA 92683
www.teachercreated.com

ISBN: 978-1-4206-3918-6

© 2014 Teacher Created Resources
Made in U.S.A.

Table of Contents

Explicit and Implicit Questions *(cont.)*

Directions: Look at the cartoon. What do you think will happen next? Is this an *explicit* or an *implicit* question? Explain.

Explicit and Implicit Questions (cont.)

Directions: Look at the cartoon below. Is the question being asked an *explicit* or an *implicit* question? Explain.

"Boy in the Pond" Questions

Directions: Use the illustration on the next page to help you answer these questions. Put an **I** on the short line after any *implicit* questions. Put an **E** on the short line after any *explicit* questions. Then answer the questions on the longer lines.

1. Is the boy in the water? _____

_____

2. What season is it? _____

_____

3. Is the tree branch broken? _____

_____

4. If the boy crawled out of the water, would the goat butt him? _____

_____

5. Is a goat standing by the pond? _____

_____

6. Will the branch fall on the boy's head? _____

_____

7. How did the boy get into the water? _____

_____

8. Why doesn't the tree have any leaves? _____

_____

9. If it rains, will leaves grow on the tree? _____

_____

10. Will the boy get into trouble? _____

_____

"Boy in the Pond" Illustration

Directions: Look at the picture. Use the illustration to answer the questions on the previous page.

"Boy in the Pond" Explanation

Below you will find a detailed explanation regarding the *implicit* or *explicit* nature of each question.

1. Is the boy in the water? _____E_____

This is an explicit question because we can see the boy in the water.

2. What season is it? _____I_____

This is an implicit question. The season (spring or summer) is hinted at by the leaves on the deciduous tree, the attire of the boy, and the recreational activity he is engaged in.

3. Is the tree branch broken? _____E_____

This is an explicit question because we can see the broken branch.

4. If the boy crawled out of the water, would the goat butt him? _____I_____

This is an implicit question. The viewer has to combine clues from the picture of the goat standing next to the pond and prior knowledge that goats often *do* butt people to arrive at a reasonable answer.

5. Is a goat standing by the pond? _____E_____

This is an explicit question because we can see the goat standing by the pond.

6. Will the branch fall on the boy's head? _____I_____

This is an implicit question. The picture suggests that the branch will fall on the boy's head because it is broken and in the process of falling, and the boy is standing directly beneath it.

7. How did the boy get into the water? _____I_____

This is an implicit question. It is implied that the boy was on the branch, that it broke, and that he fell into the water.

8. Why doesn't the tree have any leaves? _____I_____

This is an implicit question because the reason is implied by picture clues. The viewer can deduce that it is spring or summer because there are leaves on nearby trees and grass growing around the pond. The tree in question has no leaves and has brittle branches. Students will have to draw on personal knowledge regarding what it means when a tree has no leaves in the growing season.

9. If it rains, will leaves grow on the tree? _____I_____

This is an implicit question. It is implied that the tree is dead. (See the explanation for #8.) Therefore, no amount of rain will make a dead tree sprout leaves.

10. Will the boy get into trouble? _____I_____

This is an implicit question. We do not see the boy getting into trouble. The viewer has to use picture clues (The boy did something dangerous.) and draw on personal experience (Have I ever gotten into trouble for doing something dangerous?) to answer the question.

Common Core State Standards Correlation

Each passage and question in *Critical Thinking: Test-taking Practice for Reading (Grade 5)* meets one or more of the following Common Core State Standards © Copyright 2010. National Governors Association Center for Best Practices and Council of Chief State School Officers. All rights reserved. For more information about these standards, go to *http://www.corestandards.org/* or *http://teachercreated.com/standards*.

Reading: Literature	Page Correlations
Key Ideas and Details	
ELA.RL.5.1 Quote accurately from a text when explaining what the text says explicitly and when drawing inferences from the text.	21-24, 28-33, 45-51, 52-53, 62-64, 68-70
ELA.RL.5.2 Determine a theme of a story, drama, or poem from details in the text, including how characters in a story or drama respond to challenges or how the speaker in a poem reflects upon a topic; summarize the text.	21-24, 28-33, 45-51, 52-53, 62-64, 68-70
ELA.RL.5.3 Compare and contrast two or more characters, settings, or events in a story or drama, drawing on specific details in the text (e.g., how characters interact).	28-33, 45-51, 52-53, 68-70
Craft and Structure	
ELA.RL.5.4 Determine the meaning of words and phrases as they are used in a text, including figurative language such as metaphors and similes.	21-24, 28-33, 45-51, 52-53, 62-64
ELA.RL.5.5 Explain how a series of chapters, scenes, or stanzas fits together to provide the overall structure of a particular story, drama, or poem.	52-53, 62-64
ELA.RL.5.6 Describe how a narrator's or speaker's point of view influences how events are described.	21-24, 45-51, 52-53, 62-64
Range of Reading and Level of Text Complexity	
ELA.RL.5.10 By the end of the year, read and comprehend literature, including stories, dramas, and poetry, at the high end of the grades 4–5 text complexity band independently and proficiently.	All
Reading: Informational Text	
Key Ideas and Details	
ELA.RI.5.1 Quote accurately from a text when explaining what the text says explicitly and when drawing inferences from the text.	18-20, 25-27, 34-38, 39-44, 54-56, 57-61, 65-67, 71-74, 75-77
ELA.RI.5.2 Determine two or more main ideas of a text and explain how they are supported by key details; summarize the text.	25-27, 34-38, 39-44, 54-56, 65-67, 71-74, 75-77

Common Core State Standards Correlation *(cont.)*

Reading: Informational Text *(cont.)*	Page Correlations
Key Ideas and Details *(cont.)*	
ELA.RI.5.3 Explain the relationships or interactions between two or more individuals, events, ideas, or concepts in a historical, scientific, or technical text based on specific information in the text.	18-20, 34-38, 39-44, 54-56, 57-61, 65-67, 71-74, 75-77
Craft and Structure	
ELA.RI.5.4 Determine the meaning of general academic and domain-specific words and phrases in a text relevant to *a grade 5 topic or subject area*.	18-20, 25-27, 34-38, 39-44, 57-61, 65-67, 71-74, 75-77
ELA.RI.5.5 Compare and contrast the overall structure (e.g., chronology, comparison, cause/effect, problem/solution) of events, ideas, concepts, or information in two or more texts.	34-38, 68-70
Integration of Knowledge and Ideas	
ELA.RI.5.8 Explain how an author uses reasons and evidence to support particular points in a text, identifying which reasons and evidence support which point(s).	18-20, 25-27, 34-38
Range of Reading and Level of Text Complexity	
ELA.RI.5.10 By the end of the year, read and comprehend informational texts, including history/social studies, science and technical texts, at the high end of grades 4–5 text complexity band independently.	all passages
Reading: Foundational Skills	
Phonics and Word Recognition	
ELA.RF.5.3 Know and apply grade-level phonics and word analysis skills in decoding words.	all passages
Fluency	
ELA.RF.5.4 Read with sufficient accuracy and fluency to support comprehension.	all passages
Language	
Vocabulary Acquisition and Use	
ELA.L.5.4 Determine or clarify the meaning of unknown and multiple-meaning words and phrases based on grade 5 reading and content, choosing flexibly from a range of strategies.	all passages
ELA.L.5.5 Demonstrate understanding of figurative language, word relationships, and nuances in word meanings.	all passages

Process Skills

Reading-comprehension tests assess student ability in two main areas: decoding and deriving meaning. Students can expect to encounter questions that cover all of the areas outlined below on standardized assessments.

Vocabulary

Vocabulary questions on reading-comprehension tests typically ask students to identify and determine the meaning of words and word parts by employing a variety of strategies, including the following:

- Identifying synonyms, antonyms, homophones, and multiple-meaning words
- Identifying the meaning of words using prefixes and suffixes
- Using reference materials: dictionary, thesaurus, and glossary
- Using root words and word origins
- Using context clues: definition, contrast, restatement, and inference

Fiction

Reading-comprehension tests usually ask students to analyze, interpret, and/or identify the following elements of fiction:

- Characters, including their traits, feelings, beliefs, motives, and actions
- Literary devices and figurative language, including hyperbole, metaphor, analogy, anthropomorphism, alliteration, simile, personification, onomatopoeia, and idioms
- Literary elements, including plot, setting, and theme
- Poetry, including rhyme, rhythm, stanza, verse, and meter
- Genres and their characteristics, including folk and fairy tales, fiction, myths, poems, fables, fantasies, historical fiction, and chapter books

Nonfiction

Reading-comprehension tests ask students to analyze and deconstruct the following elements of nonfiction passages:

- Text structure, including compare and contrast, chronological, and cause and effect
- Author's purpose and point of view, including identifying intent and bias
- Graphic features, including graphs, tables, charts, etc.
- Sequence of events
- Main idea, supporting details, and extraneous information
- Details from the text that support ideas
- Distinction between fact and opinion; identifying fact or opinion
- Types of nonfiction and their characteristics, including biographies and autobiographies
- Summarizing a passage
- Paraphrasing the main idea

Remind students…
Explicit and implicit questions can be framed around many process skills. For example, there may be character-analysis questions that are both explicit and implicit.

Content References for Student Questions

Students can expect to find questions about the topics and the skills listed below on reading-comprehension tests. This list may be used as a reference so that students are aware, in advance, of the types of questions they may be asked. Encourage students to review this list often. Room has been provided alongside the list for notes. Ultimately, you never want students to be surprised by the type of questions that they are being asked.

Vocabulary

Decoding and Structural Analysis

- antonyms
- homophones
- multiple-meaning words
- prefixes
- suffixes
- root words
- word origins

Determining Meaning

- context clues
- definition
- compare and contrast
- restatement
- inference

Reference Materials

- dictionary
- thesaurus
- glossary

Nonfiction

Text Structure

- compare and contrast
- chronological order
- cause and effect

Author's Purpose

- point of view
- intent
- bias
- fact and opinion

Main Idea

- supporting details
- extraneous information
- paraphrasing and summarizing

Content References for Student Questions *(cont.)*

Fiction

Character Analysis

- traits
- feelings
- beliefs
- motives
- actions

Literary Devices and Figurative Language

- hyperbole
- metaphor
- analogy
- anthropomorphism
- alliteration
- simile
- personification
- onomatopoeia
- idioms

Literary Elements

- plot
  —sequence of events
  —main problem
  —conflict and resolution
- setting
- theme

Poetry

- rhyme
- rhythm
- stanza
- verse
- meter

Characteristics of Genres

- folk and fairy tales
- fiction and nonfiction
- myths
- poems
- fables
- fantasies
- historical fiction
- biographies and autobiographies
- chapter books

How This Book Is Organized

This book is organized into three tests: Test A, Test B, and Test C. Each test has 50 questions and contains a mix of the types of questions that were discussed previously. The tests are scaffolded so that the degree of assistance provided decreases with each assessment.

Test A

Test A provides students with specific and detailed guidance regarding how to approach the passages and the test questions in the form of call-out boxes along the sides of both the passage and the questions. The call-out boxes are positioned beside relevant sections of text and questions. You will notice that students are asked to determine whether some of the questions are implicit or explicit. You may instruct students to indicate their responses by using either an **E** for *explicit* or an **I** for *implicit*.

Example from Test A

Directions: Read this poem about a spider. Then answer questions 9–18.

I Am Not an Insect!

by
Julia McMeans

I am not an insect, I'm a spider of renown,
And if you say I am again, I'll turn around and bound,
And spin a web so sticky thick in strength and length and size,
With fangs and legs of bristle and my eight precision eyes!

Insects are a lowly sort, an order quite inferior.
While spiders are the kings of crawl; our creeping is superior.
We'll race across your ceiling and then hang there on a thread,
And descend along that silk until we're right above your head!

> A stanza is like the paragraph of a poem.

> As you read, notice the attitude of the spider towards insects.

10. Who is narrating this poem?

    A. an insect

    B. a poet

    C. a spider

    D. a fly

Type of Question: _____

> The narrator is the person or animal who is telling the story.

How This Book Is Organized *(cont.)*

Test B

Test B continues to provide call-out support, but there is less of it, and it is more general in nature.

Example from Test B

> **Directions:** Read the poem below. Then answer questions 23–30.
>
> ## An Emerald Is as Green as Grass
>
> by
> Cristina Rossetti
>
> An emerald is as green as grass;
>   A ruby red as blood;
> A sapphire shines as blue as heaven;
>   A flint lies in the mud.
>
> A diamond is a brilliant stone,
>   To catch the world's desire;
> An opal holds a fiery spark;
>   But a flint holds fire.

Notice the figurative language that the poet uses.

27. Which of the following is the best way to describe an opal?

   A. blue

   B. brilliant

   C. sparkly like glitter

   D. green

Make inference in order to answer this question.

Test C

Test C also provides 50 practice questions but no call-out box support. It is an opportunity for students to take a reading-comprehension assessment independently. This will give both you and your students an opportunity to see the degree to which they have internalized not only the ability to correctly identify question types, but also the specific strategies they can employ to answer the questions.

How This Book Is Organized *(cont.)*

Answer Key

The answer key at the back of this book was designed to be another teaching and learning tool for both teachers and students. While it's important for students to know which answer is correct, it is equally useful for students to understand why the other options are incorrect. This answer key provides the correct answers to the questions, identifies the types of questions being asked, and details why the other options are incorrect.

The sample below shows the answer to the question in the example for Test B on the previous page. The answer key provides the correct answer, the specific type of question asked, and when appropriate whether the question is *explicit* **E** or *implicit* **I**. It also provides a brief explanation regarding the correct answer and information regarding why the other options are incorrect. A bubble answer sheet is also provided on page 78.

Sample Answer Key Response

27. Correct Answer: C *(Interpreting Poetry)*

The poem says "An opal holds a fiery spark." Glitter is sparkly.

Incorrect Answers

A. A sapphire is usually blue.

B. A diamond is described as brilliant.

D. An emerald is green.

Test A   Name: _____

Directions: Read this passage about the Mississippi River. Then answer questions 1–8.

The Mighty Mississippi

What is over 2,000 miles long and runs from Minnesota to the Gulf of Mexico? The Mississippi River! The Mississippi River is one of the longest rivers in North America. Water from creeks and streams in 31 states flows into the mighty Mississippi!

The Geography of the River

The Mississippi River begins in Lake Itasca, Minnesota. The place where a river starts is called the *source*. The source of a river can also be called its *headwaters*.

> Take a look at the questions before you read the passage.

The Mississippi River starts as a calm, narrow stream. It is about 30 feet wide. It travels south through the middle of the United States. Water from other rivers flows into it. The rivers that flow into the Mississippi are called *tributaries*. These tributaries make the Mississippi wider and faster. Two tributaries of the Mississippi are the Missouri and Ohio Rivers. The Mississippi River is over 11 miles across at its widest point.

The amazing journey of the Mississippi ends in Louisiana, in the city of New Orleans. This is where the *mouth* of the Mississippi flows out into the Gulf of Mexico. The mouth of the Mississippi River is also the location of the Mississippi River Delta. The river's delta is an area where fertile soil gathered by the river is deposited on its long southward journey. The delta region is a large ecosystem of wetlands. Even though the Mississippi is a huge and powerful river, it is only the fourth-largest in the world.

River	Continent	Length in Miles (approximate)
Nile	Africa	4,160
Amazon	South America	4,000
Yangtze	Asia	3,964
Mississippi	North America	2,300
Rio Grande	North America	1,900

> A table can help you locate information quickly.

Test A | Name: _____

The Mighty Mississippi *(cont.)*

Communities and the River

People have been living along the banks of the river for many centuries. The river is a source of food, transportation, and recreation.

The Algonquin Indians gave the river its name. The word *Mississippi* means "father of the waters." In the 16th century, Spanish explorer Hernando de Soto became the first European explorer to reach the Mississippi. In 1803, President Thomas Jefferson bought the Louisiana Territory for the United States, and the river came with it!

Many major U.S. cities grew along the river's banks, including St. Louis, Missouri; Memphis, Tennessee; and Baton Rouge, Louisiana. In the 19th century, large steam paddleboats chugged up and down the river, transporting both people and goods. Even today, 60% of all of the grain that is exported from the United States is shipped along the Mississippi River to the Gulf of Mexico.

Questions 1–8: Select the best answer.

1. Which word is a synonym for *headwaters*?
   - **A.** mouth
   - **B.** delta
   - **C.** source
   - **D.** tributary

> Remember that synonyms are words that have the same meaning.

2. Where is the source of the Mississippi River?
   - **A.** Gulf of Mexico
   - **B.** Tennessee
   - **C.** Louisiana
   - **D.** Lake Itasca

> Use the headings to help you locate the information.

Type of Question: _____

3. What helps make the Mississippi wider?
   - **A.** tributaries
   - **B.** fertile soil
   - **C.** headwaters
   - **D.** ecosystems

> Point Right To It!

Type of Question: _____

Test A   Name: _____

The Mighty Mississippi *(cont.)*

4. What does the *mouth of the river* describe?

    A. where the river begins

    B. where the river ends

    C. all of the tributaries of the river

    D. the largest tributary of the river

> Go back to the fourth paragraph to find the meaning of *mouth*.

5. Which river is shorter than the Mississippi?

    A. the Rio Grande River

    B. the Nile River

    C. the Platte River

    D. the Amazon River

> Review the information in the table to find the correct answer.

6. Why are there many cities along the Mississippi?

    A. It is the safest place in a storm.

    B. The river provides transportation.

    C. The river provides food.

    D. Both B and C.

> Use clues from the passage plus what you know about the needs of people to make an inference.

Type of Question: _____

7. Why has the author titled this passage "The Mighty Mississippi"?

    A. He or she grew up along the banks of the river.

    B. He or she is afraid of the power of the river.

    C. It is the Algonquin name of the river.

    D. It describes the importance and size of the river.

> Think about everything you learned about the river in the passage.

Type of Question: _____

8. What percentage of grain exported from the United States is shipped along the river?

    A. 40%

    B. 60%

    C. 50%

    D. 100%

> Point Right To It!

Test A | Name: _____

Directions: Read this poem about a spider. Then answer questions 9–18.

I Am Not an Insect!
by
Julia McMeans

I am not an insect, I'm a spider of renown,
And if you say I am again, I'll turn around and bound,
And spin a web so sticky thick in strength and length and size,
With fangs and legs of bristle and my eight precision eyes!

Insects are a lowly sort, an order quite inferior,
While spiders are the kings of crawl; our creeping is superior.
We'll race across your ceiling and then hang there on a thread,
And descend along that silk until we're right above your head!

We'll creep inside your cupboards and the pages of your books.
We'll hide away in every corner, crevice, crack, and nook.
An insect couldn't match our stealth, our speed, our grace, or skill.
I have to say arachnids are really quite a thrill!

The insects I have seen are slow as honey on a spoon.
By the time they get from here to there, I could be on the moon.
Eight legs to six I must admit, it really isn't fair.
I'd beat an insect every time, as if walking on the air!

To me an insect has his place, he's nothing more than food.
They're really quite delicious broiled, baked, or simply stewed.
Scrambled insects when I wake, then a crunchy snack at three;
I'll eat bugs of any kind; I'd even eat a flea!

My favorite bug, as you all know, is called the common fly.
He's really such a silly thing, it almost makes me cry.
It doesn't take a lot of work. He glides into my web,
And struggles for a moment just before he goes to bed.

So be careful what you call me, my fine two-legged friend.
My talents and my cunning you simply cannot comprehend.
You do not want to wake and find me crawling on your skin,
Or trapped inside the kind of web that only I can spin!

> A *stanza* in a poem is like a paragraph within a poem.

> As you read, notice the attitude of the spider towards insects.

> Look for differences between spiders and insects.

> Remember that poems use figurative language like metaphors and similes to compare things.

Test A   Name: _____

I Am Not an Insect! *(cont.)*

Questions 9–18: Select the best answer.

9. How many stanzas does this poem have?

   A. 7

   B. 28

   C. 1

   D. 14

> Go back and count the number of stanzas.

10. Who is narrating this poem?

    A. an insect

    B. a poet

    C. a spider

    D. a fly

Type of Question: _____

> The narrator is the person or animal who is telling the story.

11. Which word best describes the spider in this poem?

    A. scared

    B. proud

    C. lazy

    D. friendly

> Look for clues in the poem that tell you how the spider feels about himself.

12. According to the poem, what is one difference between spiders and insects?

    A. Spiders are pretty; insects are ugly.

    B. Spiders are slow; insects are fast.

    C. Spiders have eight legs; insects have six legs.

    D. Spiders only eat grass; insects eat spiders.

Type of Question: _____

> Reread the fourth stanza to discover a stated difference between spiders and insects.

Test A Name: _____

I Am Not an Insect! *(cont.)*

13. What simile describes the speed of an insect?
    - **A.** as if walking on the air
    - **B.** slow as honey on a spoon
    - **C.** really quite a thrill
    - **D.** just before he goes to bed

    > Similies use the words *as* and *like* to compare things.

14. Why are spiders faster than insects?
    - **A.** They are smaller.
    - **B.** They have six legs.
    - **C.** They have more legs.
    - **D.** Their legs are longer.

    > Think about the anatomy of the spider and how it helps it move around.

    Type of Question: _____

15. What does the phrase *just before he goes to bed* mean?
    - **A.** just before the fly falls asleep
    - **B.** just before the fly dies
    - **C.** The spider is sleepy.
    - **D.** The fly is about to eat and kill the spider.

    > Think about what the spider is preparing to do to the fly.

16. Why do you think people may confuse spiders with insects?
    - **A.** People hate spiders and insects.
    - **B.** Scientists don't know much about insects.
    - **C.** Spiders terrify people.
    - **D.** To some people, spiders and insects look very similar.

    > Use your personal experience with insects and spiders to help determine the answer.

Test A   Name: _____

I Am Not an Insect! *(cont.)*

17. Who is the two-legged friend the spider speaks to in the last stanza?

   A. an insect

   B. another spider

   C. a person

   D. a bird

> Eliminate all options that have more than two legs, then make your best choice.

18. What does the spider give the reader in the last stanza?

   A. a compliment

   B. a joke

   C. a recipe for bugs

   D. a warning

> Go back to the last stanza to see what the spider will do.

Type of Question: _____

Test A   Name: _____

Directions: Read this passage about fostering an animal. Then answer questions 19–25.

Fostering an Animal

Many people in the United States of America have a pet. Most people have a cat or dog. There are 75 million pet dogs and 85 million pet cats in America. Most cats and dogs that live as pets have healthy lives. These animals live as members of a family. They bring happiness to the people that they live with. Not all cats and dogs are lucky enough to live with a family. Every year, millions of animals are brought to shelters. Animals are brought to shelters for many reasons:

> Take a quick look at the questions before you read the passage.

- Owners die or become sick and can no longer care for them.
- Owners lose their jobs and can't pay for food and medical care.
- Some animals get lost and can't find their way home.
- Some cats and dogs are the victims of cruelty.

> Bullet points put information in a list so it is easier to find.

It is sad to think of a cat or dog in an animal shelter. But there are many ways that people can help them. One way that people help animals is to foster them until they can find a "forever" home. When you foster an animal you take it into your home. You give the animal food. You give the animal shelter. The best thing that you give the animal is comfort. Sometimes a foster animal can be with a family for a few days. Sometimes it might be there for many months.

When animals are brought to a shelter they are frightened and sometimes have been hurt. Animals feel and fear the same as people do. This can make them act in ways that make them hard to handle. A cat may scratch. A dog might bite. It takes time for an animal to get used to a new foster family. Animals need to learn that they are safe.

People who foster cats and dogs love animals. They do not get paid for what they do. When you foster a cat or dog, it means that you are responsible for taking care of the animal. It is up to you to find that animal a forever home.

Foster families find homes for the animals by talking to friends and family members. They put up posters at grocery stores or fire stations. They use Internet sites like Petfinder and craigslist.

> Think about what a person needs to have to be a good foster parent to a cat or dog.

Many animal shelters have events where people can meet the foster pets to see if the animal will fit in with their families and the other pets they might already have.

Test A   Name: _____

Fostering an Animal *(cont.)*

Take the case of Forest. Forest is a two-year-old grey and white striped cat. He was found wandering the streets of Philadelphia on an early spring evening. He was captured by animal control workers and brought into the shelter. Forest was not wearing a collar or name tag. The people at the shelter gave him his name.

Forest was scared when he was brought into the shelter. He didn't want to be touched. His eyes were wide and he was staring at all of the people around him. The people at the shelter took care of Forest. He was examined by a veterinarian and given food, shelter, and comfort.

> Think about what kind of person would be able to help Forest.

After a few weeks, Forest was taken into foster care by Mr. Steven Rook. Mr. Rook already had four cats of his own. At first, Forest was kept in a separate room until he got used to his new environment. Eventually, Forest met Mr. Rook's other cats. He has learned to trust them and his foster dad!

"It was a long process," said Mr. Rook. "I have had Forest for almost 7 months, and he still runs under the sofa if he hears a loud noise. It must have been rough out there on the streets, but I'll take care of him until I can find him a good forever home."

Fostering a cat or dog is a great way to help animals, but it is not easy. You have to be patient with the animal. You have to pay for all of its food and medicine. You have to work hard to find the animal a safe forever home. If you can't do all of these things, then fostering a cat or dog may not be for you.

Questions 19–25: Select the best answer.

19. This passage is mostly about

    A. fostering cats and dogs.

    B. fostering farm animals.

    C. animal cruelty.

    D. animal shelters.

> Think about the entire passage, not just the introduction or conclusion.

20. How many more pet cats than dogs are in the United States?

    A. 75 million

    B. 85 million

    C. 160 million

    D. 10 million

> Go back to the first paragraph to determine the best answer.

Type of Question: _____

Test A | Name: _____

Fostering an Animal *(cont.)*

21. Which of the following is not a stated reason that animals are brought to shelters?

    A. People get sick and can't care for them.

    B. The law requires that they be brought in.

    C. People lose their jobs and can't afford them.

    D. Animals get lost.

    > Look back at the bulleted list of reasons.

22. According to the passage, what might cause a shelter cat or dog to scratch or bite?

    A. overcrowding

    B. hunger

    C. fear and pain

    D. cold temperatures

    > Look for causes and effects in paragraph 3.

Type of Question: _____

23. What is the meaning of a *forever* home?

    A. a permanent home

    B. a safe place

    C. an animal shelter

    D. a foster home

    > Look for words that are synonyms for *forever*.

24. Most likely, which animal does the author like the most?

    A. horses

    B. cats

    C. dogs

    D. puppies and kittens

    > Pay careful attention to the animal that the author writes about the most.

Type of Question: _____

25. What type of person would probably make the best foster parent for a cat or dog?

    A. a teenager

    B. a retired person

    C. a busy mom or dad

    D. a person who travels a lot for their job

    > Go back to the second half of the passage to help you answer this question.

Test A | Name: _____

Directions: Read this retelling of "The Emperor's New Clothes," by Hans Christian Andersen called "The King's Threads," and then answer questions 26–38.

The King's Threads

Not long ago, there lived a king who loved to buy new clothes. The only things he really cared about were his clothes and how good he looked in them. The king didn't care about his army. He didn't care about his citizens. He didn't care about the poor or needy. The king didn't even care about baseball! He loved clothes and that was that. Whenever anyone wanted to speak to the king about something important, he or she was told, "The king is changing his clothes. Come back later!"

> Think of other stories you know that begin this way.

The king's land was a bustling and famous kingdom. Tourists came from all over the world to visit this exciting place. One day, two con men flew into town. They told everybody they were designers of high fashion. They said that they made clothes for famous movie stars and that super models wore their clothes on the runways of Paris and New York City. But that's not all they said. They told the people they met that they had a special fabric that was invisible to anyone who was dishonest or stupid!

It wasn't long before the king found out about the two so-called designers. "Wow," the king thought, "if I had a new suit made out of that stuff, I'd be able to instantly tell the honest people from the liars and the smart from the stupid! This would make my job a whole lot easier. I'd have more time to spend on my clothes!" The king told his advisors to pay the designers $100,000 in advance for a single suit. If the king liked it, the designers were told, he'd order at least five more.

The designers brought all of their equipment to the palace. They brought work tables and sewing machines. They brought scissors, thread, patterns, and tape measures. They pretended to work very hard well into the night. But really all they did was sit around and play cards and tell each other really corny jokes.

After about a week, the king decided he wanted to have a look at the suit that the designers were making for him. But then he had a disturbing thought. "Hang on one minute. What if I can't see my own suit? I'd better get a really smart and honest person to take a look at the suit first."

> What is the king afraid of?

The king sent one of the smartest and most honest ministers to the designers. When the minister walked into the designers' workroom, he saw the two men hunched over sewing machines working on a suit that the minister could not see!

Test A | Name: _____

The King's Threads *(cont.)*

"Holy Toledo," the minister said aloud. And then he thought, "I can't see a thing." The designers asked the minister to come closer and take a good look at the suit.

"Look at the detail on this collar," said one designer. "And over here on the sleeve, do you see the intricate pattern?" asked the other.

"Of course! Of course!" lied the minister. "It is fabulous!" But the minister saw nothing but thin air.

The king called the minister to his chambers.

"Well...?" the king asked. "How's the suit coming along?"

"It is amazing!" said the minister. "The most incredible fabric I have ever laid eyes on. Really fantastic."

"Do you recommend that I order five more suits at $100,000 each?" asked the king.

"Uh, well..." the minister hesitated. He thought to himself, "If he knows that I can't see the fabric, he will think I am a dishonest simpleton. I will lose my job, my mansion, and my limo." He knew he couldn't tell the king the truth.

"Of course," said the minister. "You should definitely order at least five more."

So the king sent word to the designers, along with a check for half a million dollars.

Word soon spread about this beautiful suit that designers were making for the king and the magical powers that the fabric had. Everyone in town was waiting to find out which of their neighbors or coworkers could see the suit and which couldn't. "Now we'll all know," they thought, "who is smart and who is not, and who is honest, and who is not."

Some of the king's other ministers went to see the suit that the designers seemed to work on all day and all night. But they all had the same experience. None of them could see the suit, and every one of them lied about it.

"Is this not the most amazing suit you have ever seen?" asked one of the designers to one of the ministers.

"You've got that right," answered the minister, and all the other ministers nodded in agreement.

> Pay attention to how much information in this part of the story is unstated.

When the ministers left, the designers laughed so hard they had tears in their eyes.

"Whose turn is it to deal?" one of the designers asked the other.

Finally, the day arrived for the king to try on his new suit and parade it down the main street of the town so that everyone could see how good he looked.

Test A   Name: _____

The King's Threads *(cont.)*

"Are you sure you want to do that?" asked one of the ministers.

"Are you kidding me?" replied the king. "I spent a hundred grand on a suit, and you think I shouldn't show it off? I don't think so. Now get me that suit!"

The designers entered the king's chambers with their arms outstretched as if they were carefully carrying the suit. The ministers who stood around the king gasped. Murmurs and whispers of how fabulous the suit looked rippled through the room. Of course, no one saw a thing, including the king.

"Well, Your Highness, what do you think?" asked one of the designers. "I...uh...ahem..." the king hesitated. "What does it all mean?" he thought. "The designers can see the suit. All of my ministers can see the suit, but I cannot. This can only mean one thing. I am a dishonest fool! But I mustn't let on."

"It is," and the king paused for emphasis, "the most incredible suit that's ever been made!" So the king removed all of his clothes and allowed the designers to fit him into his new, magical suit. After the designers were finished, the king turned to look at himself in the mirror. "Oh dear," the king thought, "I am completely naked."
"How do I look?" the king asked.

"Sire," said the designers and all of the ministers, "you look marvelous."

> Why does everyone pretend to see the suit?

The king walked outside with his ministers following behind.
As he paraded down the main street of the town, people came to their doors and windows. Cars and buses slowed down in the street. People stopped texting, tweeting, and Facebooking to get a good look at the king in his new suit. "Oh, my!" exclaimed the townsfolk. "Isn't the king's suit fantastic?"

Of course, no one could see a single shred of thread. All anyone saw was a naked king strolling down the middle of the road, but no one admitted it. After a time, a child standing on the parade route with his father yelled, "Dad! Hey, Dad! Look at the king! He's naked!" Silence descended over the crowd. The king stopped dead in his tracks. Then the boy's father started to laugh.

"Didn't I tell you, Sammy, to stop telling all those lies?"

The father turned toward the king. "Excuse him, Your Majesty. You know what little boys are like." The king acknowledged the father with a nod of his head and then moved on past the boy.

The boy's father grabbed him by the hand and pulled him away from the crowd. All the while the boy protested, saying, "But Dad, he's naked. The king is really naked!"

And as the boy and his father turned a corner, they saw the designers jumping into the car of a fast-moving train.

Test A | Name: _____

The King's Threads (cont.)

Questions 26–38: Select the best answer.

26. What kind of story is "The King's Threads"?

    A. fiction

    B. nonfiction

    C. myth

    D. fairy tale

> More than one answer may be correct. Select the most specific one.

27. Which adjective do you think best describes the king?

    A. jealous

    B. vain

    C. intelligent

    D. wicked

> Remember, an adjective is a word that describes.

Type of Question: _____

28. How much does a single suit cost?

    A. $500,000

    B. $50,000

    C. $10,000

    D. $100,000

> Check the third paragraph.

Type of Question: _____

29. Why do the ministers make the designers laugh?

    A. They pretend to see the suit.

    B. They told a corny joke.

    C. They were naked.

    D. They tickled them.

> Think about what is happening as they are laughing.

30. Why did the king send his minister to see the suit first?

    A. He doubted his own intelligence and honesty.

    B. The king is too important to do such things.

    C. The king feared the designers.

    D. The minister asked to go.

> Implicit questions often begin with the word *why*.

Type of Question: _____

Test A | Name: _____

The King's Threads *(cont.)*

31. The phrase "Holy Toledo" in paragraph 7 is

  A. a simile

  B. a metaphor

  C. an anagram

  D. an idiom

> Use the process of elimination to help determine the answer.

32. Why can't anyone see the suit that the designers have made?

  A. It is invisible.

  B. They are liars and fools.

  C. They are honest and smart.

  D. There really isn't a suit.

> The answer to this question is implied by the text. Read between the lines.

Type of Question: _____

33. According to the story, if you said that you couldn't see the suit, it would mean that

  A. you are truthful and smart.

  B. you are dishonest and a fool.

  C. you don't like the king.

  D. you don't want to hurt the king's feelings.

> Remember, it suggests two separate things.

34. Why were the designers able to get away with their con?

  A. Because no one was willing to speak the truth.

  B. Because the king had all of the power.

  C. Because the suit itself was magical.

  D. Because the king threatened them.

> Think about the behavior of the characters.

35. Who is the only person in the story to tell the truth?

  A. the boy's father

  B. the boy

  C. a designer

  D. a minister

> Point Right To It!

Type of Question: _____

Test A | Name: _____

The King's Threads *(cont.)*

36. Why is the boy not afraid to tell the truth about the king's suit?

    A. The boy is too young to fear what adults think about him.

    B. The boy is not very bright.

    C. The boy's father put him up to it.

    D. The boy is really the son of the king.

> Use what you know about children plus clues from the story to make an inference.

37. Why don't the designers stay for the parade?

    A. They are too busy playing cards.

    B. They are busy making the king more suits.

    C. They overslept.

    D. They want to get out of town before they are found out.

> Think about what the designers got away with.

38. Which of the following best describes the theme of this story?

    A. Vanity will get you nowhere.

    B. Honesty is the best policy.

    C. Con men always win.

    D. Think for yourself, or else you may look foolish.

> Think about how the characters' behavior makes them look.

Test A   Name: _____

Directions: Read this passage called "Frogs and Toads." Then answer questions 39–50.

Frogs and Toads

Have you ever heard that if you kiss a frog, it might turn into a prince? This, of course, is a myth about frogs. There is nothing magical about frogs, but they are quite an impressive species.

Frogs are amphibians. An *amphibian* is an animal that can live on the land and in the water. The word *amphibian* means "double life." Most animals live either on the land like elephants, or they live in the water like whales. Amphibians, like frogs, have the best of both worlds!

> Skim the passage and diagram before you begin to read.

There are over 4,000 different species of frogs. Many frogs are green, but there are lots of frogs that are red, blue, and even yellow. Some frogs, like the poison dart frog, can be dangerous. The dart frog secretes a type of poison through its skin. This discharge can be harmful. Native people used to put the frog poison on tips of their arrows. This is how dart frogs got their name.

Most frogs are nocturnal and are rarely seen during the day. Frogs are carnivorous. They eat a diet that is mainly insects. Frogs use the sticky tip of their tongues to grab their food. Of course, there are many people in the world, especially in France and in China, who eat frog legs and consider them a delicacy.

> What does it mean if an animal is *nocturnal*?

The skin of a frog is moist and smooth. Frogs have webbed feet. And although you may never have seen them, frogs have teeth! Frogs are great jumpers.
This is because they have very strong back legs. The Australian tree frog can jump 50 times the length of its body. That is over six feet! This jumping ability makes the frog a superior animal.

Toads are very much like frogs, but there are some important differences:

- Toads become more *terrestrial* as they age, spending most of their lives on the ground.

- Toads have rough, dry skin that is bumpy.

- Toads have no teeth, and their back legs are not nearly as strong as the legs of a frog.

- Toads have two poison glands that are positioned behind their eyes.

- A female toad can lay about 4,000 to 12,000 eggs per year. (Like frogs, toad eggs are laid in clusters in the water.)

Test A | Name: _____

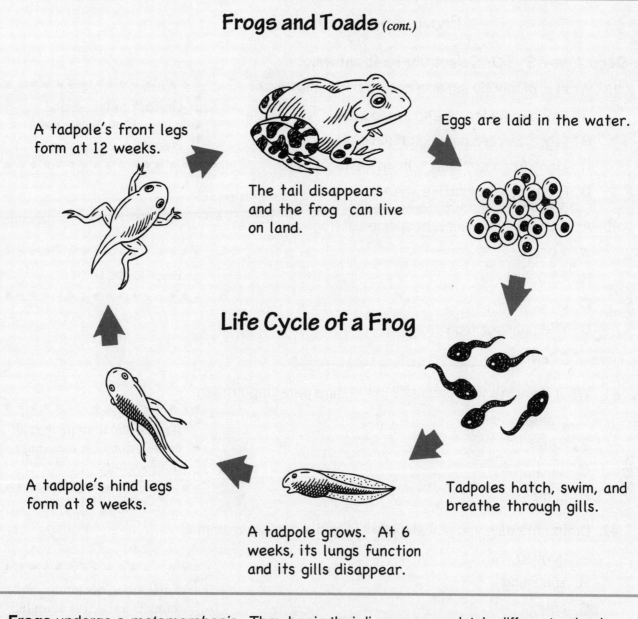

Frogs and Toads *(cont.)*

A tadpole's front legs form at 12 weeks.

The tail disappears and the frog can live on land.

Eggs are laid in the water.

Life Cycle of a Frog

Tadpoles hatch, swim, and breathe through gills.

A tadpole grows. At 6 weeks, its lungs function and its gills disappear.

A tadpole's hind legs form at 8 weeks.

Frogs undergo a *metamorphosis*. They begin their lives as completely different animals. Frogs start out as tadpoles. Over the course of about 80 days they transform into frogs. A female frog can lay about 18,000 to 20,000 eggs per year. Female frogs lay their eggs in clusters in the water.

One of the most recognizable features of a frog is the croaking sound it makes. This is how frogs communicate with one another. Frogs croak to attract mates and to warn other frogs of their presence.

Test A   Name: _____

Frogs and Toads *(cont.)*

Questions 39–50: Select the best answer.

39. What is meant by the frog having a "double life"?

    A. Frogs mate for life and live in pairs.

    B. Frogs can live on land and in water.

    C. Many frogs are born with an identical twin.

    D. Frogs have a long life span.

> Go back to the second paragraph to locate the answer.

40. About how many different species of frogs are there?

    A. 4,000

    B. 40,000

    C. 50

    D. The passage didn't say.

> Point Right To It!

Type of Question: _____

41. What does the word *secretes* in the third paragraph mean?

    A. creates

    B. hides

    C. discharges

    D. combines

> Review the third paragraph to determine the meaning of this word.

42. During the day, you would expect to find a nocturnal animal

    A. hunting.

    B. spawning.

    C. eating.

    D. resting.

> Remember, nocturnal animals are active at night.

Type of Question: _____

43. A food that is a *delicacy* is probably

    A. high in calories.

    B. very tasty.

    C. bland.

    D. inexpensive.

> Use what you know about base words to answer this question.

Test A | Name: _____

Frogs and Toads *(cont.)*

44. Why do you think frogs have webbed feet?

    A. to help them swim.

    B. to help them catch flies.

    C. to help them spawn.

    D. to help them jump.

> Think about the environment in which frogs live.

Type of Question: _____

45. Why is the statement "this jumping ability makes frogs a superior animal" an opinion?

    A. Frogs are not good jumpers.

    B. There are other animals that can jump as well.

    C. This is something people could disagree about.

    D. Everyone would agree with the statement.

> Remember, an opinion can't be proven with facts.

46. What does the word *terrestrial* mean?

    A. nocturnal

    B. ground dwelling

    C. pond dwelling

    D. insect eating

> Look for clues in the sentence to figure out what the word means.

47. How are toads different from frogs?

    A. Toads have teeth; frogs do not.

    B. Frogs are green; toads are brown.

    C. Frogs begin as tadpoles; toads do not.

    D. Frogs have teeth; toads do not.

> Point Right To It!

| Test A | Name: _____ |

Frogs and Toads *(cont.)*

48. What happens to tadpoles when they are about eight weeks old?

    A. They hatch from eggs.

    B. They form hind legs.

    C. Their tail shrinks.

    D. Their external gills disappear.

Type of Question: _____

> Use the diagram to help answer this question.

49. What do tadpoles use to breathe?

    A. gills

    B. lungs

    C. fins

    D. frungs

> Examine the life cycle of a frog on the diagram. Read all of the captions.

50. What adaptations allow the frog to live on the land?

    A. lungs and smooth skin

    B. lungs and front legs

    C. front and back legs

    D. gills and lungs

Type of Question: _____

> Think about what is necessary for survival out of the water.

Test B   Name: _____

Directions: Read this passage called "The Maya." Then answer questions 1–11.

The Maya

Let's play a guessing game. Read the following words and try to guess what this passage is all about. Are you ready? Here we go. The first word is *pyramids*. Did you instantly think about the ancient Egyptians? I thought you would. Let's try another word. The word is *glyphs*. Ancient Egyptians again, right? This passage is not about the ancient Egyptians. Let's try another word. The word is *chocolate*. Can you guess? I will give you one more clue.

The clue is the name of a place. The place is Central America. Are you thinking what I'm thinking? If you're thinking Maya, then we think alike!

> Scan the subheadings before you read the passage.

Maya Cities

The Maya lived about fifteen hundred years ago. They lived in the area that we call Central America. This area is also called Mesoamerica. The prefix *meso* means "in the middle." The Maya were great builders. They built 70 cities. These cities had populations between 5,000 and 50,000 people. If you look at the map, you can see where many of the important Maya cities were located.

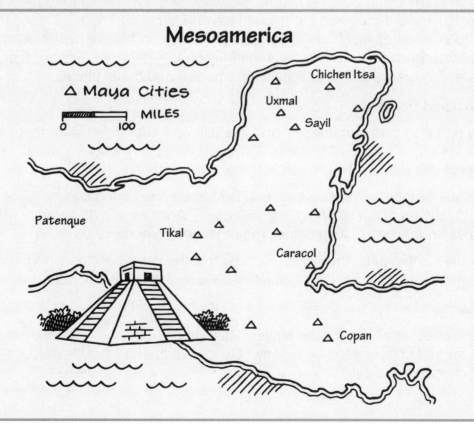

Mesoamerica

△ Maya Cities

0 — 100 MILES

Chichen Itsa

Uxmal

Sayil

Patenque

Tikal

Caracol

Copan

Test B   Name: _____

The Maya *(cont.)*

Maya Ballcourts

Most Maya cities had a ballcourt in town. Usually, the court would be built at the foot of a temple. The courts were shaped like a capital letter *I*. The ballcourts had tiers of bleachers. They looked a lot like our sports stadiums. People from the surrounding villages would come to the big city to watch the game.

> Look for reasons why Maya ball isn't always fair.

The game the Maya played was a rough sport. On either side of the court there were hoops made of stone. The Maya players tossed around a hard, rubber ball. The goal was to get the rubber ball into the hoop. You could use your hips, shoulders, and arms to move the ball around.

Sometimes the teams were not evenly matched. On one side there would be a team of professional ballplayers. The other team would be made up of Indians that the Maya captured. These players were confined and not given very much food. They often lost the game. Losing meant that you could be used in the ritual of human sacrifice!

Pyramids

The Maya are famous for building pyramids. Many of them still stand today. Archaeologists have discovered the ruins of several Maya pyramids. They excavate the areas to uncover as much of the pyramids as they can. Maya pyramids have carvings of their gods. The pyramids of the Maya had a different purpose than those of Egyptians. They were used for religious ceremonies and burial places.

Maya Math and Science

The Maya had their own number system. It is different than the system that we use. The Maya system is a base 20 system. Ours is base ten. The Maya were one of the first people to use a zero. They even had a *glyph*, or symbol, for it.

The Maya are famous for their calendar. It is different than our calendar. The Maya use three calendars. One calendar has 260 days. Another has 365 days. The third is called the *calendar round*. It combines the other two calendars.

Some people believed that the Maya calendar told the day when the world would end. That date was December 21st, 2012, the last date on the Maya calendar.

Chocolate

Do you love chocolate? So did the Maya! They drank hot chocolate as part of a religious ceremony. Check out this Maya hot-chocolate recipe!

> What word gives you a clue that something is not factual?

Test B Name: _____

The Maya *(cont.)*

Maya Hot Chocolate

Ingredients

4 cups of milk

$\frac{1}{2}$ cup unsweetened cocoa powder

1 tsp. flour

$\frac{1}{4}$ cup brown sugar

3 cloves, crushed

$\frac{1}{4}$ tsp. nutmeg

1 cinnamon stick (broken into pieces)

$\frac{1}{4}$ tsp. dried, crushed chili peppers

2 tsp. powdered confectioner's sugar

1 $\frac{1}{2}$ tsp. vanilla extract

cornstarch (optional)

Directions

1. Over low heat, heat the milk in a double boiler on the top of the stove.

2. Sift the cocoa powder and the flour together and slowly stir in enough hot milk to make a paste.

3. Add the remaining ingredients to the paste and stir the entire mixture into the hot milk in the double boiler. Stir constantly to keep the mixture from burning.

4. Stir in a little cornstarch if you want thicker hot chocolate. Add a little at a time until the hot chocolate is the desired consistency.

5. Remove the cloves and cinnamon pieces with a slotted spoon.

6. Add the vanilla extract and powdered sugar.

7. Serve hot in mugs.

Test B   Name: _____

The Maya *(cont.)*

Questions 1–11: Select the best answer.

1. Which word best describes the tone of the introductory paragraph?

   A. serious

   B. fun

   C. sad

   D. confusing

Look for clues that reveal the tone of the passage.

Type of Question: _____

2. Why is Central America most likely called Mesoamerica?

   A. because it is one of the Americas

   B. because *meso* means "central"

   C. because the area is in the middle of North and South America

   D. because the area is in the center of North America

Think about the meaning of the prefix *meso*.

3. Which of the following is not a Maya city?

   A. Tikal

   B. Copan

   C. Sayil

   D. Chiapas

Look carefully at the map to find the answer.

Type of Question: _____

4. The Maya ball game can best be compared to

   A. basketball.

   B. baseball.

   C. tennis.

   D. hockey

Use clues from the passage along with what you know about sports to find the best answer.

Type of Question: _____

Test B   Name: _____

The Maya *(cont.)*

5. Why were some ball games unfair?

   A. The Maya liked to cheat.

   B. The king decided the winner.

   C. Play would end as soon as someone got hurt.

   D. The Maya played people who were weaker and didn't even know the game.

> Go back and reread the section about the Maya ballcourts. A and D seem similar.

6. What did the Maya use pyramids for?

   A. tombs and ball games

   B. religious ceremonies and ball games

   C. religious ceremonies

   D. stargazing

> Point Right To It!

7. The passage says that archaeologists excavate the area of the pyramids. The word *excavate* means

   A. to dig up.

   B. to cover.

   C. to study.

   D. to rebuild.

> Go back to the passage and read the word in context to figure out what it means.

8. What is a *calendar round*?

   A. a kind of sundial

   B. a calendar with 260 days

   C. a combination of two calendars

   D. a calendar with 365 days

> Point Right To It!

Type of Question: _____

Test B | Name: _____

The Maya *(cont.)*

9. Which of the following is an opinion?

    A. This is because the Maya calendar stops counting on that date.

    B. The date is December 21ˢᵗ, 2012.

    C. The Maya are famous for their calendar.

    D. The Maya calendar tells the day when the world will end.

> Remember the difference between a fact and an opinion.

10. Which of the following is not an ingredient for Maya hot chocolate?

    A. cream

    B. milk

    C. nutmeg

    D. vanilla extract

> Reread the list of ingredients.

11. The recipe states that cornstarch is optional. What does *optional* mean?

    A. necessary

    B. is added last

    C. expensive

    D. not necessary

> Look for a root word that can help you determine the meaning.

Test B | Name: _____

Directions: Read this passage called "Lewis and Clarke Practice Math." Then answer questions 12–22.

Lewis and Clarke Practice Math

It was one of those kinds of perfect weather days in the middle of May. The sun was bright, and the sky was deep blue. Puffy, white clouds punctuated the blue canopy just so things didn't get too boring. The breeze was warm and gentle. The old oak trees surrounding Franklin Middle School were covered in tiny buds that would soon burst out into full-blown leaves, and the early spring daffodils and tulips were already giving way to a bouquet of early summer blooms.

On a day like this, fifth-grader Patrick Lewis felt extremely unlucky. He was imprisoned in his math class by Mr. Bone, the hardest math teacher on the entire planet. And he was sitting next to an open window. Poor Patrick could feel the warm spring breeze on his cheek, hear the buzzing bees in his ears, and smell that indefinable odor that only spring can bring.

"And how do we convert twenty-four hundredths into a decimal?"

Mr. Bone was addressing Patrick. But poor Patrick was staring out of the window wishing he were on his bike.

Look for details that describe the setting.

"Ahem.... I say, hello, Patrick, come in, Patrick."

Suddenly, Patrick snapped out of his trance to discover Mr. Bone standing over him. His classmates chuckled under their breath.

"Twenty–four hundredths into a decimal, eh, Patrick. What do you say?"

But Patrick didn't say a thing. He hadn't a clue how to answer the question, so he just shrugged his shoulders.

Mr. Bone moved on.

"Anyone?" he asked the class.

Of course, Brandon Bragg's hand shot up in the air like a sail on a windy day.

"It's point twenty-four, Mr. Bone," Brandon responded. Then he turned and gave Patrick a smirk.

Patrick let out a long sigh and quickly looked down at his desk. He stayed that way until the bell rang.

The truth of the matter was that Patrick Lewis and math just didn't get along. Patrick didn't know his median from his mode, a scatter plot from a scalene triangle, or a function from a fact family. A big part of the problem was that because Patrick didn't like math, he didn't spend too much time studying or practicing it. He always did just enough to pass, but not enough to do well.

The situation was getting bleaker by the minute because the math kept getting harder and harder, and Patrick kept getting lazier and lazier. The worst part was that he had to take one more giant, end-of-the-year math exam. He was barely getting a C right now. If he didn't ace the math final, it would be curtains!

Test B   Name: _____

Lewis and Clarke Practice Math *(cont.)*

Of course, making things even harder was Patrick's dad. Professor Lewis was a rocket scientist; a real rocket scientist, so he was very good at math.

"I just don't get it," Professor Lewis, said to his colleague, Dr. Newton, as he found the slope of a tangent line using mental math. "Math comes so naturally to me. I just thought it would for Patrick, too."

Patrick's favorite thing to do was to read. He loved poems and stories. He read science fiction and fantasy novels. Once, he read *Harry Potter and the Order of the Phoenix* in three days!

> What is the problem in the story?

Things got so bad for Patrick that Mr. Bone asked Dr. Lewis to come in for a parent-teacher conference.

"The problem," Mr. Bone explained, "is that young Patrick spends all of his time staring out of the window and reading books about wizards and flying horses."

"Yes," replied Professor Lewis. "He reads all of the time. My Patrick is quite a voracious reader."

"I am," Patrick piped in. "I once read *Harry Potter and the Order of the Phoenix* in three days! That book is 870 pages long!"

"That's 12.08 pages per hour," said Mr. Bone.

"Indeed, Bone, indeed," responded Professor Lewis. "But that is based on 24 hours per day. I do think Patrick slept some of the time."

"Sure…" Patrick said slowly.

"So based on reading, oh, let's say eight hours per day," Professor Lewis calculated, "that gives us a reading rate of 36 and a quarter pages per hour."

"Of course, Professor," replied Mr. Bone, "of course."

Patrick just shrugged and sighed. What are they talking about?

Mr. Bone and Professor Lewis came up with a plan which involved setting Patrick up with a peer tutor. They thought that if Patrick could study with someone his own age, he might be more willing to try harder and learn his math.

The following day, Patrick walked into the school library and spotted Barry Clarke seated at a table by himself with the fifth-grade math textbook opened up in front of him.

"Oh no! Patrick thought. "Barry Clarke is a math genius. What a nightmare." As Patrick approached the table, he noticed Barry put an empty bag of gummy bears in his pocket.

Test B | Name: _____

Lewis and Clarke Practice Math *(cont.)*

"Hey," Patrick said, and sat down.

Patrick dug his books out of his book bag. Barry noticed that Patrick had a Hogwarts sticker on the flap of his bag.

"Chaser, Beater, Seeker, or Keeper?" Barry asked excitedly.

"Huh?" replied Patrick, retrieving a pencil.

"Chaser, Beater, Seeker, or Keeper?" Barry insisted.

"Oh," Patrick said smiling. "Beater, I think. You?"

"Keeper. I'd like to play Seeker," Barry said as he grabbed a bit of his belly, "but I don't have the build for it."

"Well," Patrick said, "without a good Keeper, you're nothing."

Maybe this won't be so bad after all, he thought.

Barry explained all of the math basics to Patrick, going over stuff that Patrick didn't understand.

"The thing about math," Barry said, "is you just have to practice a lot."

"Yeah, I know. But I don't practice because I don't seem to be very good at it. I always get the wrong answer."

"Really? What is the house number of the Order of the Phoenix Headquarters on Grimmauld Place multiplied by the number of the Dementors that attacked Harry and Dudley at the beginning of the Order of the Phoenix?"

"What?" Patrick asked.

"You heard. What's the answer?"

"Uh, oh, well, the address is twelve, twelve Grimmauld Place times two Dementors equals 24. The answer is 24."

"Correct," said Barry. "If four of Harry's wands make up the sides of a square, what would the perimeter be?"

"Hang on…well, Harry's wand is 11 inches…"

"Yes…" said Barry.

"And the perimeter is the distance around…"

| Test B | Name: _____ |

Lewis and Clarke Practice Math *(cont.)*

"The formula," Barry said, "is perimeter equals two times the length plus two times the width. You don't have any gummy bears do you?"

"Forty-four!" cried Patrick.

"Fantastic! You have forty-four gummy bears," Barry said and held out his hand.

"No," laughed Patrick. "The answer to your question is forty-four."

When Patrick returned home that day, his dad asked him how his tutoring went.

"Great!" replied Patrick. "We talked about Harry Potter the entire time."

For the next two weeks Patrick and Barry, or as they began to call themselves, Lewis and Clarke, met in the library and studied for the math test. Well, most of the time they studied.

Sometimes they debated which Harry Potter book was the best, or how awesome it would be if J.K. Rowling wrote just one more book. Occasionally, Barry would sneak a gummy bear, even though they weren't supposed to eat in the library.

The day of the test came and went. Barry got an A+, naturally. Patrick got a B–.

"B– is pretty good for somebody who doesn't like math," Barry said.

"Not too bad," Patrick said, handing Barry a package of gummy bears. "Thanks for your help."

"No biggie," Barry said, tearing open the gummy packet with his teeth.

"We should still meet up, even though we don't have to study for math anymore," Patrick said.

"Great idea," replied Barry. "So let me ask you something."

"No more math questions, please," begged Patrick.

"What would you do if you bumped into a Dementor?"

> How is the problem in the story solved?

Test B | Name: _____

Lewis and Clarke Practice Math *(cont.)*

Questions 12–22: Select the best answer.

12. What is the setting of the story?

   A. a middle school

   B. Patrick's bedroom

   C. Hogwarts

   D. the library

> Point Right To It!

13. Which of the following is an example of *hyperbole*?

   A. The situation was getting bleaker by the moment.

   B. If he didn't ace the math test, it would be curtains.

   C. Of course, Brandon Bragg's hand shot up in the air like a sail on a windy day.

   D. He was imprisoned in his math class by the hardest teacher on the entire planet, Mr. Bone.

> Eliminate options that you know are wrong.

14. What was Patrick doing when Mr. Bone called on him in class?

   A. sleeping

   B. chatting with another student

   C. daydreaming

   D. working out the answer to the question

> Go back to the story to find out what Patrick was doing.

Type of Question: _____

Test B   Name: _____

Lewis and Clarke Practice Math *(cont.)*

15. Which word(s) do you think best describes Brandon Bragg?

    A. shy

    B. know-it-all

    C. scaredy cat

    D. none of these

> Think about Brandon's behavior.

Type of Question: _____

16. Which of the following is a *simile*?

    A. puffy, white clouds punctuated the blue canopy

    B. hand shot up in the air like a sail on a windy day

    C. hardest math teacher on the entire planet

    D. We talked about Harry Potter the whole time.

> Remember the structure of a simile.

17. What is the problem in this story?

    A. Patrick reads too many Harry Potter books.

    B. Barry eats too many gummy bears.

    C. Patrick is not good at math, and he has to pass a big test.

    D. Mr. Bone is an unfair teacher who picks on Patrick.

> Think about what is bothering Patrick.

18. Professor Lewis refers to Patrick as being a voracious reader. What does the word *voracious* mean?

    A. slow and plodding

    B. eager

    C. occasional

    D. reads in the dark

> Go back to the story and read the paragraph that contains this word.

Test B   Name: _____

Lewis and Clarke Practice Math *(cont.)*

19. The phrase "it would be curtains" is an example of

    A. a metaphor.

    B. onomatopoeia.

    C. an analogy.

    D. an idiom.

> Use the process of elimination to find the answer.

20. Why doesn't Patrick understand part of the conversation between his dad and Mr. Bone?

    A. because math confuses him

    B. because they are adults

    C. because he is daydreaming

    D. because he has his fingers in his ears

> Go back and reread this part of the story.

Type of Question: _____

21. Why do you think Patrick and Barry refer to themselves as Lewis and Clarke?

    A. They don't know each other's first names.

    B. They have the same names as two famous explorers.

    C. It is the rule of Franklin Middle School.

    D. They don't know each other.

> Make a deduction.

22. Why do Patrick and Barry get along so well?

    A. They are both great at math.

    B. They both love Harry Potter books.

    C. They are both in Mr. Bone's class.

    D. They both love gummy bears.

> Think about what the characters have in common.

Test B | Name: _____

Directions: Read the poem below. Then answer questions 23–30.

An Emerald Is as Green as Grass

by
Cristina Rossetti

An emerald is as green as grass;
A ruby red as blood;
A sapphire shines as blue as heaven;
A flint lies in the mud.

A diamond is a brilliant stone,
To catch the world's desire;
An opal holds a fiery spark;
But a flint holds fire.

> Notice the figurative language that the poet uses.

Questions: 23–30: Select the best answer.

23. What type of figurative language is present in the first stanza of the poem?

   A. hyperbole

   B. personification

   C. simile

   D. alliteration

> Read each option before you select one.

24. What is the rhyme scheme of the poem?

   A. aabb

   B. abcb

   C. abcd

   D. baba

> Circle words that rhyme to help you see the pattern.

25. Which stanza tells where the flint can be found?

   A. first

   B. second

   C. first and second

   D. neither

> Go back to the poem and locate the word.

Type of Question: _____

Test B | **Name:** _____

An Emerald Is as Green as Grass *(cont.)*

26. According to the poem, which stone would people want the most?

    A. flint

    B. opal

    C. ruby

    D. diamond

> Reread the poem.

27. Which of the following is the best way to describe an opal?

    A. blue

    B. brilliant

    C. like glitter

    D. green

> Make an inference in order to answer this question.

28. Which stone does the poet suggest is the most useful?

    A. flint

    B. diamond

    C. sapphire

    D. all of the stones mentioned

> Think about what the poet says about each stone.

Type of Question: _____

29. What is meant by *a flint holds fire*?

    A. A flint stone can spark a fire.

    B. A flint stone is as bright as fire.

    C. A flint stone feels hot.

    D. A flint stone is made from fire.

> Think about how the stones are used.

30. Which of the following best describes the poem's theme?

    A. The most precious stones are those that are beautiful.

    B. The most precious stones are those that are useful.

    C. Shiny stones are the most precious.

    D. Useful things can't be beautiful.

> What is the message of the poem?

| Test B | Name: _____ |

Directions: Read the passage called "The Jobs of Steve Jobs." Then answer questions 31–38.

The Jobs of Steve Jobs

Steve Jobs was a great American inventor. He was the co-founder of Apple. He died of cancer in 2011. He was 56.

Great inventors make things that change how people live. Thomas Edison invented the electric light. That invention meant that people no longer had to live by the rising and setting sun. Henry Ford found a way to make cars that people could afford. Before the car, most folks used a horse and buggy. After Ford's invention, people could travel twice as far in half the time. Cars and electric lights transformed the world.

> Think about the characteristics of inventors.

Steve Jobs and his partner Steve Wozniak also made something that changed how people live. They figured out how to build a computer that could be used in the home. Before this, computers were huge machines. They took up lots of space and not that many people knew how to use them. Computers were used by the military. They helped launch rockets into space. Before the 1970s, no one had one in their house. Now, many homes in America have computers!

Steve Jobs was born in California in 1955. He met his friend, Woz, in middle school. They were both interested in computers. They got summer jobs at a computer company called Hewlett-Packard. After high school, Jobs attended Reed College for a short time. A few years later, Jobs worked for Atari. Atari made some of the first computer games. He and his old school friend, Woz, helped to create a circuit board that used less chips, or parts. The fewer the chips, the smaller the device. A smaller game unit was easier to handle and cheaper to produce.

In 1979, the two friends started their own company. They called it Apple. Steve Jobs was a big fan of the Beatles. The Beatles had a record company called Apple. Jobs admired that there were four Beatles who worked together to make something great. Jobs believed in teamwork. He named his company after theirs. The logo for Apple Records is a green apple. The famous logo for Apple computers is an apple with a bite taken out of it.

> Who is Steve Jobs and what did he accomplish?

Apple is the company that brought the first personal computer to the American market. It was called the Apple II. It went on sale in 1977. Apple didn't invent the computer. They were the first to bring an affordable computer that could be mass produced for *everyday* people.

Test B Name: _____

The Jobs of Steve Jobs (cont.)

This is very similar to what Henry Ford did. He did not invent the car. He figured out a way to make a good car cheaply and quickly. By the end of 1980, one hundred thousand Apple II's had been sold. The computer age was underway.

The Apple II computer was the first of many new products that Jobs and his company developed. The iPhone, iPad, and iPod were also created by Apple.

To be a great inventor you have to have a great imagination. Steve Jobs is often called a visionary. A *visionary* is a person who can imagine a future that others cannot. Can you imagine what life would be like if you didn't have a small computer on which to surf the net? How about that iPod you listen to on your way to and from school? And what about the iPhone that lets you listen to music, take pictures, browse the Internet, text, and play games? What do you think Edison and Ford would think of these inventions?

Steve Jobs was not born rich or famous. He went to public schools. He did not finish college. His many inventions made him rich and famous, but these were not the most important things to him. Steve Jobs once said, "Being the richest man in the cemetery doesn't matter to me… going to bed at night saying we've done something wonderful… that's what matters to me." And what Steve Jobs did mattered. It mattered very much.

Questions 31–38: Select the best answer.

31. To whom does the author compare Steve Jobs?

    A. Benjamin Franklin

    B. Alexander Graham Bell

    C. George Washington Carver

    D. Thomas Edison

    Point Right To It!

    Type of Question: _____

32. Which of the following activities would have been easier to do after the invention of the electric light?

    A. sleep

    B. read

    C. tell stories

    D. feed your horse

    Make an inference.

    Type of Question: _____

Test B   Name: _____

The Jobs of Steve Jobs (cont.)

33. What or who is "Woz"?
    A. the nickname of the Apple II
    B. Steve Wozniak
    C. the Apple I
    D. Steve Jobs

> Read all the options before you choose.

34. What innovation did the two Steves develop at Atari?
    A. They made the circuit board smaller.
    B. They made the circuit board more complex.
    C. They made the circuit board that was used by the military.
    D. They made the first computer game.

> Go back to the passage and reread this paragraph.

Type of Question: _____

35. According to the passage, how are Steve Jobs and Henry Ford alike?
    A. They both dropped out of college.
    B. They both have many patents.
    C. They are both American.
    D. They both made new technology affordable to the average person.

> You'll have to look in more than one place to find the answer.

36. According to the passage, how are the Beatles and Steve Jobs connected?
    A. They are cousins.
    B. Steve Jobs named his company after theirs.
    C. The Beatles wrote a song about Steve Jobs.
    D. iTunes sells Beatles songs.

> Select the best answer to this question.

37. What was the name of the first personal computer?
    A. Apple II
    B. Apple I
    C. Atari
    D. Hewlett-Packard

> Go back to the passage to find the answer.

38. How did people search the Internet before the Apple II?
    A. They used the Apple I.
    B. They went to the library.
    C. There was no Internet as we know it at that time.
    D. They used their iPhones.

> Draw a conclusion.

Test B | Name: _____

Directions: Read the passage called "Hawk Mountain." Then answer questions 39–50.

Hawk Mountain

Hawk Mountain is a bird refuge in Pennsylvania. A *refuge* is a place that protects the health and safety of a type of animal. These places are created because some animals are threatened by hunting. Sometimes, animals are endangered because of the loss of the environment they depend on for their survival.

> Skim the passage and questions first.

Hawk Mountain protects birds of prey. Raptors, hawks, and bald eagles are all birds of prey. This means that they hunt and eat other small animals for food. These birds are also hunted by people. This is the main reason that the sanctuary at Hawk Mountain was started.

History of Hawk Mountain

In the 1920s, people thought of birds of prey differently than they do nowadays. Hawks and vultures were considered pests. Back then, the state government would pay hunters to shoot them out of the sky. Thousands and thousands of birds were killed this way. Now we know that all animals have a *niche*, or a special job to do. Birds of prey keep the population of rodents and other small animals balanced.

> How did Hawk Mountain become a refuge?

In 1929, a man named Richard Plough discovered that hunting was taking place at Hawk Mountain. He came to the mountain one day and gathered all of the dead birds that the hunters were paid to kill. He laid them out on the forest floor and took pictures of them. His photographs *caught the eye* of Rosalie Edge.

Mrs. Edge was a conservationist. She believed that the natural world should be protected from things like over-hunting. Mrs. Edge leased over 1,000 acres of Hawk Mountain. She put a warden on the land to make sure that hunting of the birds stopped. Soon after, she bought the land and created the first bird sanctuary in the United States.

Bird Watching at Hawk Mountain

People come from all over to see the birds at Hawk Mountain. They bring binoculars and cameras to watch and photograph them. Almost anytime you can see falcons and vultures soar over the mountaintop and swoop down deep into the valley.

Test B   Name: _____

Hawk Mountain *(cont.)*

The people who work at Hawk Mountain keep a count of the birds that are spotted there every day.

Hawk Mountain Migration Counts 10/15/11			
Bird Type	**Today's Count**	**Season Count to Date**	**Highest Daily Count this Season**
Black Vulture	2	8	6
Red-tailed Hawk	14	278	62
Sharp-shinned Hawk	21	2,186	266
Rough-legged Hawk	0	0	0

Hiking at Hawk Mountain

Bird watching isn't the only fun thing to do at Hawk Mountain. There are lots of trails on which you can hike and get great views of the birds and the surrounding mountain. Some of the trails on the mountain are good for folks who don't want to do a lot of climbing. But there are plenty of trails for people who want to dig in and really break a sweat!

All of the trails on Hawk Mountain are color-coded. This means that as you walk on the trail, you will see colored blaze marks on the trees that show you the way so you don't get lost. For example, the Lookout Trail is also the orange trail. This is a great walk for young children, moms and dads with strollers, or maybe your grandparents. It is one mile long. You can get some fantastic views of the thousand trees that blanket the mountain on this trail.

The River of Rocks Trail Loop is the red trail. This trail is extremely rocky, so you really have to watch your footing as you walk. It descends about 600 feet down the mountain. If you're not in the mood for a tricky hike that takes about three hours to complete, then this may not be the trail for you.

Test B   Name: _____

Hawk Mountain *(cont.)*

The Golden Eagle Trail, a yellow blaze trail, will really make you work! It may be only two miles long, but it has a vertical rise of 800 feet. Once you get to the top, you can pick up the Skyline Trail and follow the blue blazes. This trail is not for the fainthearted. It requires the hiker to climb over the ridge top of the mountain. The ridge top is nothing but a series of huge boulders. It is also at an elevation of about 1,500 feet. This trail connects to the famous Appalachian Trail.

Other Activities at Hawk Mountain

Hawk Mountain offers all kinds of fun activities. They have lectures, egg hunts, and native-plant gardens. They also have classes where you can learn all about the different types of birds that the sanctuary protects.

So, if you are ever in western Pennsylvania and you want to meet a turkey vulture or a falcon face-to-face, then visit Hawk Mountain.

Questions 39–50: Select the best answer.

39. Where is Hawk Mountain?

    A. Virginia

    B. Pennsylvania

    C. Hawk Valley

    D. New York

Type of Question: _____

> Point Right To It!

40. Which word is a synonym for *refuge*?

    A. zoo

    B. sanctuary

    C. park

    D. hospital

> Go back to the story to find a synonym for *refuge*.

Test B   Name: _____

Hawk Mountain *(cont.)*

41. A bird of prey would probably eat

    A. a horse.

    B. insects.

    C. grass and other plants.

    D. a chipmunk.

Type of Question: _____

> Look for clues in the story to help you make a deduction.

42. What might happen if the population of birds of prey was greatly diminished?

    A. The population of small rodents would increase.

    B. The population of small rodents would decrease.

    C. The vegetation on the mountain would become overgrown.

    D. Hunters would lose their jobs.

Type of Question: _____

> Make an inference.

43. What does the idiom *caught the eye* mean?

    A. to get poked in the eye

    B. to take a photograph

    C. to be a conservationist

    D. to get a person's attention

> Remember what an idiom is.

44. A warden is very similar to

    A. a newspaper reporter.

    B. a school principal.

    C. a police officer.

    D. a veterinarian.

> Think about the duties of a warden.

45. How many sharp-shinned hawks were spotted on October 15th?

    A. 2

    B. 21

    C. 0

    D. 4

Type of Question: _____

> Review the table to find the answer.

Test B   Name: _____

Hawk Mountain (cont.)

46. What is the highest daily count for the red-tailed hawk?

　　A. 266

　　B. 6

　　C. 278

　　D. 62

....
Review the table.
....

47. What is the purpose of blaze marks?

　　A. The color tells you how difficult a trail is.

　　B. They mark the trail so you don't get lost.

　　C. They point the way to the best bird viewing.

　　D. They prevent forest fires.

Type of Question: _____

....
Point Right To It!
....

48. Why do people think the Lookout Trail is good for young children and older people?

　　A. It is a challenging hike.

　　B. It is an easy hike.

　　C. It has lots of benches.

　　D. It has fantastic views.

Type of Question: _____

....
Draw a conclusion.
....

49. What makes the Golden Eagle Trail so difficult?

　　A. You have to climb up 800 feet.

　　B. You have to climb down 800 feet.

　　C. You have to climb over the ridge of the mountain.

　　D. It is an elevation of 1,500 feet.

....
Go back to the paragraph that mentions this trail.
....

50. Which trail connects to the Appalachian Trail?

　　A. Skyline Trail

　　B. Golden Eagle Trail

　　C. Blaze Trail

　　D. River of Rocks Trail

....
Go back to the passage to find the answer.
....

Test C   Name: _____

Directions: Read the poem, "The Land of Nod," by Robert Louis Stevenson. Then answer questions 1–10.

The Land of Nod

by

Robert Louis Stevenson

From breakfast on through all the day
At home among my friends I stay,
But every night I go abroad
Afar into the land of Nod,

All by myself I have to go,
With none to tell me what to do—
All alone beside the streams
And up the mountain-sides of dreams.

The strangest things are there for me,
Both things to eat and things to see,
And many frightening sights abroad
Till morning in the land of Nod.

Try as I like to find the way,
I never can get back by day,
Nor can remember plain and clear
The curious music that I hear.

Questions 1–10: Select the best answer.

1. How many stanzas are in the poem?

   A. 1

   B. 2

   C. 16

   D. 4

2. Where is the land of Nod located?

   A. in another country

   B. in another town

   C. in the narrator's head

   D. abroad

Test C | Name: _____

The Land of Nod *(cont.)*

3. What is the rhyme scheme of this poem?

  A. abab

  B. aabb

  C. abcd

  D. bbaa

4. What is the narrator of the poem really describing?

  A. a hospital

  B. his dreams

  C. his bedroom

  D. a strange country abroad

5. Why can't the narrator take anyone with him on his travels?

  A. He likes to travel alone.

  B. No one wants to go with him.

  C. You can't take people to the land of your own dreams.

  D. It is against the rules.

6. How does the narrator describe the land of Nod?

  A. exciting

  B. boring

  C. cold

  D. strange

Test C   Name: _____

The Land of Nod *(cont.)*

7. How do you return from the land of Nod?

   A. You wake up.

   B. You take a train or boat.

   C. You have to walk alone.

   D. You have to climb the mountain-sides of dreams.

8. Why can't the narrator find his way to the land of Nod during the day?

   A. His parents won't allow it.

   B. He can't find the stream that takes him there.

   C. You have to be asleep at night to get there.

   D. He can't hear the music he has to follow to get there.

9. In the last two lines of the poem, the narrator is really describing

   A. how hard it is to remember your dreams.

   B. how poor his memory is.

   C. how confused his dreams are.

   D. how much he dislikes the music he hears in his dreams.

10. Which of the following words best describes the tone of the poem?

   A. funny

   B. terrifying

   C. haunting

   D. sarcastic

Test C   Name: _____

Directions: Read the passage about composting. Then answer questions 11–20.

How to Make Compost

Everybody knows that plants can make their own food. Plants use the process of photosynthesis to make the food they need to survive. But what about the soil in which these plants grow? How do we keep it rich in the nutrients that the plants need?

There are many products that you can buy at the garden center that feed plants and keep the soil nutritious. But there is an even better way that is good for the environment, too. Why not create your very own compost heap?

Compost is organic matter that has decomposed. Once that happens, it can be used as fertilizer. Organic matter is anything that was once alive, so it is easy to find. Compost needs two basic elements, nitrogen and carbon, which can be found in many everyday things. To make your own compost, just follow these easy directions.

Compost Directions

1. Choose a dry, elevated, sunny spot in your backyard or at a community garden. It should be about 4 feet by 8 feet.

2. Begin the first layer of your compost. Combine dried leaves, grass clippings, and twigs.

3. Every few days, add more organic material to the pile. Add vegetable and fruit peels, coffee grounds, straw, and eggshells.

4. You can also add shredded newspaper or computer paper.

5. Do not add meat, oils, animal waste, dairy, or plants that have been treated with weed killers to your compost.

6. If you don't receive much rain, add a little water to the compost to keep it moist.

7. Once a week, turn over the compost with a shovel to mix it up.

8. Cover the whole pile with a trash bag.

9. In about 4 to 6 months, your compost will be ready.

Composting is a great way to feed plants. It is natural and chemical free. It is also good because when you compost, you are recycling and creating less waste from things that you use. Composting is good for plants and people.

Test C Name: _____

How to Make Compost *(cont.)*

Questions 11–20: Select the best answer.

11. What process do plants use to make their own food?

    A. photosynthesis

    B. compost

    C. nutrient production

    D. osmosis

12. Which of the following is not an example of organic matter?

    A. banana

    B. spider

    C. leather purse

    D. pen

13. What are the two basic chemical ingredients in compost?

    A. carbon and oxygen

    B. carbon and hydrogen

    C. carbon and nitrogen

    D. nitrogen only

14. Which of the following would be a good location for a compost heap?

    A. under a tree

    B. next to a creek

    C. in a ditch

    D. none of these

Test C   Name: _____

How to Make Compost *(cont.)*

15. The first layer of your compost should have

    A. eggshells and coffee grounds.

    B. shredded newspapers.

    C. weed killer.

    D. grass clippings and twigs.

16. Which of the following should not be added to the compost?

    A. eggshells

    B. cheese

    C. fruit peels

    D. straw

17. What should you do to the compost on a weekly basis?

    A. Turn it over with a shovel.

    B. Add water to it.

    C. Take the plastic trash bag off.

    D. Treat it with weed killer.

18. Why is paper considered organic matter?

    A. because it is made from something that is dead

    B. because it is recyclable

    C. because it can be shredded

    D. because it comes from trees that were once alive

19. Which of the following best describes how compost should be maintained?

    A. It should be kept dry.

    B. It should be kept cool.

    C. It should be kept away from the sun.

    D. It should be kept moist.

20. How does the compost reduce waste?

    A. Things that we would throw away are being reused.

    B. No chemicals are being consumed.

    C. They don't take up as much space as recycling containers.

    D. It's all organic.

Test C   Name: _____

Directions: Read the story called "Sam the Magnificent." Then answer questions 21–30.

Sam the Magnificent

Sam is a fifth-grade student at Elm Street Elementary School. Not long ago, he read a biography about a famous magician called Harry Houdini. Houdini is one the most famous magicians that ever lived. He was born over a hundred years ago. One of the things he became famous for was being able to escape from almost anything.

One of Houdini's most daring escapes was called the Milk Can Escape. For this trick, Houdini had his hands and feet handcuffed. Then, he would have himself locked inside of a large milk container. Back in those days, these containers were like big metal barrels. Houdini would have the barrel filled with water and then tightly sealed and locked. Houdini, of course, always managed to escape. No one really knew how he did this trick, but it was this trick that made him famous. Over the years, Houdini performed many amazing escapes from locked wooden crates and other kinds of containers.

After reading about Houdini, Sam wanted to become a magician. He read all sorts of books about how to perform different types of magic. He taught himself how to do tricks with coins and cards. But there was one trick that he did that left everyone amazed. Sam called it *Pick a Number.*

Sam's father came home one evening and Sam said to him, "Hey, Dad, pick a number from one to five."

"Okay, Sam, how about two?"

Sam said, "Two it is! Now, go over and lift up the cushion of the couch."

Sam's dad lifted up the cushion and found a little piece of paper.

"Now," Sam said, "read what is on that piece of paper."

Sam's dad carefully unfolded the piece of paper.

"What's it say?" asked Sam, smiling.

"It says, 'I knew you would pick two!'"

Sam's dad just stood there for a minute. Finally, he said, "How did you know I would pick two?

"It's magic," said Sam.

Later on that evening, Sam performed the same trick for his mother. His mom picked number five.

Test C   Name: _____

Sam the Magnificent *(cont.)*

"Mom, go over and look underneath that stack of magazines."

Sam's mom found a tiny piece of paper. When she unfolded it she read, "I knew you would pick five!"

"How did you do that?" asked Sam's mom. "You must be psychic! It's as if you can read my mind!"

But Sam couldn't read anyone's mind. And there is no magic involved at all. Can you figure out how Sam knew in advance what numbers his parents would select?

Questions 21–30: Select the best answer.

21. Who is the main character of the story?

   A. Houdini

   B. Sam

   C. Sam's father

   D. Sam's mother

22. Who is Houdini?

   A. a famous teacher

   B. Sam's father

   C. a famous magician

   D. a former senator

23. What is Houdini famous for being able to do?

   A. card tricks

   B. tricks using coins

   C. great feats of strength

   D. amazing escapes

24. Which of the following best describes how Sam feels about Houdini?

   A. He is inspired by him.

   B. He is afraid of him.

   C. He is annoyed by him.

   D. He is jealous of him.

Test C **Name:** _____

Sam the Magnificent *(cont.)*

25. What is the name of Sam's famous magic trick?

    A. Milk Can Escape

    B. Handcuff Escape

    C. Houdini Classic

    D. Pick a Number

26. Which of the following best describes the Milk Can Escape?

    A. Houdini was locked in a wooden chest.

    B. Houdini was handcuffed and locked in a wooden chest.

    C. Houdini was handcuffed and locked in a large milk container.

    D. Milk containers are made to disappear.

27. How many numbers can you choose from in Sam's trick?

    A. 5

    B. 3

    C. 10

    D. 2

28. On whom did Sam first perform his trick?

    A. his friend Harry

    B. his mom

    C. his uncle

    D. his dad

29. What does the trick make it look like Sam can do?

    A. guess what people are thinking

    B. guess where something is hidden

    C. pull a rabbit out of a hat

    D. make an amazing escape from a box

30. Why do you think Sam does not tell his parents how the trick is done?

    A. He is angry with them.

    B. Magicians don't tell their secrets.

    C. He can't explain it.

    D. He is a little spoiled.

Test C Name: _____

Directions: Read the passage called "Sam's *Pick a Number* Trick." Then answer questions 31–40.

Sam's *Pick a Number* Trick

Want to learn how to impress your teachers, parents, and friends? Are you looking for a way to make them believe that you are a skilled magician with psychic abilities? Want them to walk away scratching their heads in wonderment? Well, look no further, my friends. Here is a trick that you can play that will leave them stunned and amazed! Follow these easy steps, and you are on your way to becoming the most famous *prestidigitator* (that's a fancy word for *magician*) in your neighborhood.

Instructions for *Pick a Number*

Step 1: Get five small rectangular pieces of paper.

Step 2: On the first piece of paper, write the following: "I knew you would pick 1."

Step 3: On the second piece of paper write, "I knew you would pick 2."

Step 4: Repeat this process with numbers 3, 4, and 5.

Step 5: Now, take the numbered pieces of paper and hide them around your house or classroom. For example, hide the paper that says, "I knew you would pick 1," under a sofa cushion. Hide the paper that says, "I knew you would pick 2," under a plant pot.

Most Important! Make sure no one sees you doing this! You can set the trick up days before you plan on doing it!

Step 6: Make sure you remember where you hid each piece of paper.

Step 7: Wait for an opportunity when the trickee (That's the person being tricked!) is in the room where you hid the numbered papers.

Step 8: Ask this person to pick a number from 1 to 5. Don't look around the room when you ask.

Step 9: Let's say that the trickee selects number 3.

Step 10: Remember where you hid the piece of paper that says, "I knew you would pick 3," (perhaps you hid it under a plant pot) and say to the trickee, "Go look under the plant pot."

| Test C | Name: _____ |

Sam's *Pick a Number* Trick *(cont.)*

Instructions for *Pick a Number* *(cont.)*

Step 11: When the trickee retrieves the paper, instruct him or her to read it. Of course, the trickee will read, "I knew you would pick 3."

Step 12: No doubt the trickee will now say something like, "Wow! How did you know I would pick 3?"

Step 13: The truth is you did not know the trickee would say 3. But you did know where you hid the paper that says, "I knew you would pick 3." From the point of view of the trickee, if looks as if you read his or her mind!

Step 14: No matter how much the trickee asks how you did it, don't tell! A magician never reveals the secrets to his or her tricks!

Questions 31–40: Select the best answer.

31. What is a *prestidigitator*?

   A. an escape artist

   B. the trickee

   C. the trickster

   D. a magician

32. Why do you need five pieces of paper to perform this trick?

   A. Five numbers are involved.

   B. Five is an odd number.

   C. There are five fingers on each hand.

   D. Five is half of ten.

33. Which of the following might you find written on one of the pieces of paper?

   A. "I saw you!"

   B. "Gotcha!"

   C. "I knew you would pick 4."

   D. "You can't fool me!"

Test C | Name: _____

Sam's *Pick a Number* Trick *(cont.)*

34. Who is the *trickee?*

    A. the person performing the trick

    B. the person being tricked

    C. the magician

    D. the prestidigitator

35. Why is it important that no one sees you hiding the pieces of paper?

    A. So they can't find them.

    B. You may get into trouble.

    C. If they see you, then they will be able to figure out the trick.

    D. none of these

36. What do you do in Step 8?

    A. Invite the trickee into the room.

    B. Tell the trickee to look under the plant pot.

    C. Hide the pieces of paper.

    D. Ask the trickee to pick a number from one to five.

37. What is the most important part of this trick?

    A. remembering where you hid the pieces of paper

    B. writing clearly on the pieces of paper

    C. selecting good hiding places

    D. explaining the trick to the trickee

| Test C | Name: _____ |

Sam's *Pick a Number* Trick *(cont.)*

38. What might cause this trick to fail?

    A. selecting bad hiding places

    B. forgetting where you hid the papers

    C. not knowing the magic words

    D. performing the trick on a really smart person

39. Most likely, why would you only use five numbers in this trick?

    A. Five is most magicians' lucky number.

    B. So you can do this trick with little kids.

    C. It would take too long to do it with larger numbers.

    D. It would be hard to remember more than five hiding places.

40. Why would you not be able to perform this trick twice in a row?

    A. because you need time to set up the trick

    B. because it would be too exhausting

    C. No one would want to see it twice in a row.

    D. all of these

Test C   Name: _____

Directions: Read the passage called "Edible Insects!" Then answer questions 41–50.

Edible Insects!

In the United States of America, insects, more commonly know as "bugs," are not seen as food items. But this is not the case in many places in the world. In countries all over the globe, many people eat insects. In fact, raising and eating insects as food has a name. It is called *entomophagy*. The prefix *ento* means insect!

People munch on all sorts of insects. Ants, mealworms, butterflies, beetles, and grasshoppers are just some of the protein-rich, yummy buggies that people eat. Here is a recipe for some delicious cookies!

Chocolate Chip Cicada Cookies

Ingredients

3 cups of flour
1 teaspoon baking soda
1 teaspoon of salt
1½ cups softened butter
¾ cup of sugar
¾ cup of brown sugar
1 teaspoon of vanilla
3 eggs
1 12-ounce bag of semi-sweet chocolate chips
1 cup of chopped walnuts
¾ cup of roasted, salted cicadas

Directions

1. Preheat the oven to 375 degrees.
2. In a small bowl, mix the flour, baking soda, and salt.
3. In a large bowl, combine the butter, sugar, brown sugar, and vanilla. Beat until creamy.
4. In a small bowl, crack the eggs and beat them with a fork.
5. Add the eggs to the butter mixture.
6. Gradually add the flour mixture to the sugar mixture until completely blended.
7. Stir in the chocolate chips, walnuts, and the cicadas.
8. Drop rounded, measured tablespoons of dough onto an ungreased cookie sheet.
9. Bake for 8–10 minutes.

Test C   Name: _____

Edible Insects! *(cont.)*

Questions 41–50: Select the best answer.

41. What does the word *edible* mean?

    A. insect

    B. something that can be eaten by people

    C. something that is usually not eaten by people

    D. recipe

42. Identify the prefix in the word *entomophagy*.

    A. phagy

    B. mophagy

    C. en

    D. ento

43. What is the name of the insects in the cookie recipe?

    A. chips

    B. cicadas

    C. mealworms

    D. grasshoppers

44. How much salt is used in the recipe?

    A. 1 teaspoon

    B. 3 teaspoons

    C. ¾ of a teaspoon

    D. 1 tablespoon

45. Why do you think the recipe calls for softened butter?

    A. Softened butter has a better taste.

    B. Softened butter is easier to mix and stir.

    C. Softened butter works better with insect recipes.

    D. The author of the recipe prefers softened butter.

Test C   Name: _____

Edible Insects! *(cont.)*

46. How many cicadas does the recipe call for?

   A. ¾ of a cup

   B. about a handful

   C. 10

   D. 3

47. What do you do right before you add the eggs to the butter mixture?

   A. add the flour to the butter mixture

   B. stir in the chocolate chips and cicadas

   C. preheat the oven

   D. crack the eggs in a small bowl and beat them

48. If you bake the cookies for 12 minutes, what would probably happen?

   A. They would probably burn.

   B. They would probably be undercooked.

   C. The cicadas would die.

   D. They would be perfectly cooked.

49. Which type of cicadas does the recipe call for?

   A. sugar-coated cicadas

   B. live cicadas

   C. roasted, salted cicadas

   D. cicada larvae

50. How do you think most people would feel after eating a cookie, if they were not told beforehand that they were eating a cicada?

   A. silly

   B. sad

   C. annoyed

   D. bored

Name: _____ Date: _____

Bubble Answer Sheet   Test _____

1. Ⓐ Ⓑ Ⓒ Ⓓ

2. Ⓐ Ⓑ Ⓒ Ⓓ

3. Ⓐ Ⓑ Ⓒ Ⓓ

4. Ⓐ Ⓑ Ⓒ Ⓓ

5. Ⓐ Ⓑ Ⓒ Ⓓ

6. Ⓐ Ⓑ Ⓒ Ⓓ

7. Ⓐ Ⓑ Ⓒ Ⓓ

8. Ⓐ Ⓑ Ⓒ Ⓓ

9. Ⓐ Ⓑ Ⓒ Ⓓ

10. Ⓐ Ⓑ Ⓒ Ⓓ

11. Ⓐ Ⓑ Ⓒ Ⓓ

12. Ⓐ Ⓑ Ⓒ Ⓓ

13. Ⓐ Ⓑ Ⓒ Ⓓ

14. Ⓐ Ⓑ Ⓒ Ⓓ

15. Ⓐ Ⓑ Ⓒ Ⓓ

16. Ⓐ Ⓑ Ⓒ Ⓓ

17. Ⓐ Ⓑ Ⓒ Ⓓ

18. Ⓐ Ⓑ Ⓒ Ⓓ

19. Ⓐ Ⓑ Ⓒ Ⓓ

20. Ⓐ Ⓑ Ⓒ Ⓓ

21. Ⓐ Ⓑ Ⓒ Ⓓ

22. Ⓐ Ⓑ Ⓒ Ⓓ

23. Ⓐ Ⓑ Ⓒ Ⓓ

24. Ⓐ Ⓑ Ⓒ Ⓓ

25. Ⓐ Ⓑ Ⓒ Ⓓ

26. Ⓐ Ⓑ Ⓒ Ⓓ

27. Ⓐ Ⓑ Ⓒ Ⓓ

28. Ⓐ Ⓑ Ⓒ Ⓓ

29. Ⓐ Ⓑ Ⓒ Ⓓ

30. Ⓐ Ⓑ Ⓒ Ⓓ

31. Ⓐ Ⓑ Ⓒ Ⓓ

32. Ⓐ Ⓑ Ⓒ Ⓓ

33. Ⓐ Ⓑ Ⓒ Ⓓ

34. Ⓐ Ⓑ Ⓒ Ⓓ

35. Ⓐ Ⓑ Ⓒ Ⓓ

36. Ⓐ Ⓑ Ⓒ Ⓓ

37. Ⓐ Ⓑ Ⓒ Ⓓ

38. Ⓐ Ⓑ Ⓒ Ⓓ

39. Ⓐ Ⓑ Ⓒ Ⓓ

40. Ⓐ Ⓑ Ⓒ Ⓓ

41. Ⓐ Ⓑ Ⓒ Ⓓ

42. Ⓐ Ⓑ Ⓒ Ⓓ

43. Ⓐ Ⓑ Ⓒ Ⓓ

44. Ⓐ Ⓑ Ⓒ Ⓓ

45. Ⓐ Ⓑ Ⓒ Ⓓ

46. Ⓐ Ⓑ Ⓒ Ⓓ

47. Ⓐ Ⓑ Ⓒ Ⓓ

48. Ⓐ Ⓑ Ⓒ Ⓓ

49. Ⓐ Ⓑ Ⓒ Ⓓ

50. Ⓐ Ⓑ Ⓒ Ⓓ

Master Answer Sheet for Tests A, B, and C

Answers for Test A (pages 18–38)

1. C	6. D	11. B	16. D	21. B	26. D	31. D	36. A	41. C	46. B
2. D	7. D	12. C	17. C	22. C	27. B	32. D	37. D	42. D	47. D
3. A	8. B	13. B	18. D	23. A	28. D	33. B	38. D	43. B	48. B
4. B	9. A	14. C	19. A	24. B	29. A	34. A	39. B	44. A	49. A
5. A	10. C	15. B	20. D	25. B	30. A	35. B	40. A	45. C	50. B

Answers for Test B (pages 39–61)

1. B	6. C	11. D	16. B	21. B	26. D	31. D	36. B	41. D	46. D
2. C	7. A	12. A	17. C	22. B	27. C	32. B	37. A	42. A	47. B
3. D	8. C	13. D	18. B	23. C	28. A	33. B	38. C	43. D	48. B
4. A	9. D	14. C	19. D	24. B	29. A	34. A	39. B	44. C	49. A
5. D	10. A	15. B	20. A	25. A	30. B	35. D	40. B	45. B	50. A

Answers for Test C (pages 62–77)

1. D	6. D	11. A	16. B	21. B	26. C	31. D	36. D	41. B	46. A
2. C	7. A	12. D	17. A	22. C	27. A	32. A	37. A	42. D	47. D
3. B	8. C	13. C	18. D	23. D	28. D	33. C	38. B	43. B	48. A
4. B	9. A	14. D	19. D	24. A	29. A	34. B	39. D	44. A	49. C
5. C	10. C	15. D	20. A	25. D	30. B	35. C	40. A	45. B	50. C

Test A Answer Key

1. C	6. D	11. B	16. D	21. B	26. D	31. D	36. A	41. C	46. B
2. D	7. D	12. C	17. C	22. C	27. B	32. D	37. D	42. D	47. D
3. A	8. B	13. B	18. D	23. A	28. D	33. B	38. D	43. B	48. B
4. B	9. A	14. C	19. A	24. B	29. A	34. A	39. B	44. A	49. A
5. A	10. C	15. B	20. D	25. B	30. A	35. B	40. A	45. C	50. B

Explanations for Test A Answers

The Mighty Mississippi (pages 18–20)

1. **Correct Answer: C** *(Vocabulary)*
   Source and *headwaters* have the same meaning, so they are synonyms.
   Incorrect Answers:
   A. *Mouth* and *headwaters* are antonyms.
   B. A river's *delta* and *headwaters* are not the same.
   D. A river's *tributary* and *headwaters* are not the same.

2. **Correct Answer: D** *(Locating Details)* E
   The passage clearly states that the Mississippi begins at Lake Itasca.
   Incorrect Answers:
   A. The Gulf of Mexico is the river's mouth.
   B. The river does not start in Tennessee.
   C. The river does not start in Louisiana.

3. **Correct Answer: A** *(Locating Details)* E
   The passage clearly states that tributaries make the river wider and faster.
   Incorrect Answers:
   B. Fertile soil does not make the river wider.
   C. Headwaters refer to the source of the river.
   D. Ecosystems are not related to the width of the river.

4. **Correct Answer: B** *(Using Context to Determine Meaning)*
   Where a river ends is the same as its mouth.
   Incorrect Answers:
   A. Where the river begins is the source.
   C. The tributaries are small creeks, streams, or rivers that flow into it.
   D. A large tributary is not the same as the mouth of the river.

5. **Correct Answer: A** *(Interpret Graphic Features: Table)*
   According to the table, the Rio Grande (1900 miles) is shorter than the Mississippi.
   Incorrect Answers:
   B. The Nile is 4,160 miles. It is longer.
   C. The Platte is not on the table.
   D. The Amazon is 4,000 miles. It is longer.

6. **Correct Answers: D** *(Locating Details)* I
   The passage states that the river provides both transportation and food.
   Incorrect Answers:
   A. The passage does not say anything about safety.
   B. The passage clearly states that the river provides transportation, but this is not the best answer.
   C. The passage clearly states that the river provides food, but this is not the best answer.

7. **Correct Answer: D** *(Analyzing Author's Purpose)* I
   The title conveys the power, size, and historical importance of the river.
   Incorrect Answers:
   A. There is nothing in the passage to suggest that the author grew up near the river.
   B. There is nothing in the passage to suggest that the author fears the river.
   C. *Mississippi* is the Algonquin name for the river, not *Mighty Mississippi.*

8. **Correct Answer: B** *(Locating Details)*
   The passage states that 60% of exported grain in the U.S. is transported along the Mississippi River.
   Incorrect Answers:
   A. Forty percent is not stated anywhere in the passage.
   C. Fifty percent is not stated anywhere in the passage.
   D. One-hundred percent is not stated anywhere in the passage.

Explanations for Test A Answers (cont.)

I Am Not an Insect! (pages 21–24)

9. **Correct Answer: A** *(Identifying Characteristics of Poetry)*
By counting the stanzas, you can identify seven.
Incorrect Answers:
- **B.** The poem does not have 28 stanzas.
- **C.** The poem does not have one stanza.
- **D.** The poem does not have 14 stanzas.

10. **Correct Answer: C** *(Interpreting Poetry)* **E**
The poem states "I'm a spider of renown."
Incorrect Answers:
- **A.** The narrator is not an insect. The narrator doesn't like insects.
- **B.** The poet and the narrator are not the same things.
- **D.** The fly is the victim of the spider narrator.

11. **Correct Answer: B** *(Interpreting Poetry)*
The poem implies that the narrator is proud and thinks he is superior to insects.
Incorrect Answers:
- **A.** The poem implies that the narrator is not afraid. He or she is a predator, fearing nothing.
- **C.** The poem implies that the narrator is not lazy. He or she is industrious, spinning webs and crawling quickly.
- **D.** The poem implies that the narrator is not friendly. He or she preys on other insects and threatens readers.

12. **Correct Answers: C** *(Locating Details)* **E**
The poem clearly states that one difference between insects and spiders is the number of legs they have.
Incorrect Answers:
- **A.** The poem does not address prettiness or ugliness.
- **B.** The poem states the opposite of this: Spiders are fast, and insects are slow.
- **D.** The poem states that spiders eat flies.

13. **Correct Answer: B** *(Interpreting Figurative Language: Simile)*
This is a simile because it compares the speed of an insect to honey on a spoon and uses the word *as*.
Incorrect Answers:
- **A.** This is a simile, but it describes the speed of a spider.
- **C.** This is not simile.
- **D.** This is a metaphor. It compares sleeping to death directly.

14. **Correct Answer: C** *(Making Inferences)* **I**
The spider has two more legs than an insect. You can infer that more legs equal more speed.
Incorrect Answers:
- **A.** There is nothing here to imply that a spider is smaller than an insect.
- **B.** Insects have six legs, and spiders have eight.
- **D.** There is no information in the poem that says that a spider has longer legs than an insect.

15. **Correct Answer: B** *(Interpreting Figurative Language: Metaphor)*
The metaphor compares going to sleep with the permanent sleep of death.
Incorrect Answers:
- **A.** This is the literal, not the figurative, interpretation.
- **C.** The spider is not sleepy. He is waiting attentively for the fly to glide into his web.
- **D.** Flies do not eat or kill spiders. Spiders eat flies.

16. **Correct Answer: D** *(Interpreting Poetry)*
People often can't see the subtle differences among other species of animals. Creatures with more than two legs that crawl tend to look the same from the human perspective.
Incorrect Answers:
- **A.** Hating something is not a reason to confuse it with something else.
- **B.** This is a false statement. Scientists know much about insects.
- **C.** Spiders do frighten some people, but fear is not likely to make some confuse one type of animal for another.

17. **Correct Answer: C** *(Making Inferences)*
The spider is speaking to another living thing that has cupboards, books, and two legs. People are the only animals that have all of these things.
Incorrect Answers:
- **A.** Insects have six legs.
- **B.** Spiders have eight legs.
- **D.** Birds have two legs but *not* cupboards and books.

18. **Correct Answer: D** *(Interpreting Poetry)* **I**
The spider threatens to crawl on a person or to trap a person by spinning a web around him or her.
Incorrect Answers:
- **A.** The spider does not say anything nice to or about the reader.
- **B.** The spider's tone is menacing, not humorous.
- **C.** While the spider likes to eat bugs, there is not a specific recipe here.

Explanations for Test A Answers *(cont.)*

Fostering an Animal *(pages 25–27)*

19. Correct Answer: A *(Identifying the Main Idea)*
Fostering cats and dogs is a great way to provide temporary food, shelter, and kindness until the animal can find a permanent home.

Incorrect Answers:

B. There is no mention of farm animals in the passage.

C. Animal cruelty is mentioned, but it is not the main idea of the passage.

D. The passage talks about the important work of animal shelters, but shelters themselves are not the main idea of the passage.

20. Correct Answer: D *(Making Inferences)* **E**
You must subtract the number of pet dogs from the number of pet cats.

Incorrect Answers:

A. There are 75 million pet dogs in the U.S.

B. There are 85 million pet cats in the U.S.

C. 160 million is the number of pet dogs and cats combined.

21. Correct Answer: B *(Locating Supporting Details)*
The passage does not address the legality of bringing animals to shelters.

Incorrect Answers:

A. Illness of pet owners is an explicitly stated reason that animals are brought to shelters.

C. Inability to afford a pet is stated as a reason that animals are brought to shelters.

D. Animals getting lost is stated as a reason that animals are brought to the shelter.

22. Correct Answer: C *(Locating Supporting Details)* **E**
The passage states that when animals are brought to the shelter, they are often frightened and hurt.

Incorrect Answers:

A. Overcrowding is not given as a cause for scratching or biting.

B. Shelter animals may be hungry, but this is not stated as a cause for scratching or biting.

D. Cold temperatures may be uncomfortable for animals, but this is not given as a reason for aggressive behavior.

23. Correct Answer: A *(Determining Meaning: Inference)*
Paragraph 2 states the foster animals may stay with families for a few days or many months. The paragraph implies that the animal's stay is temporary until a permanent home can be found.

Incorrect Answers:

B. Safety is a characteristic of a forever home, but it is not the literal meaning.

C. An animal shelter is a temporary placement for the cat or dog.

D. A foster home is the opposite of a forever home.

24. Correct Answer: B *(Identifying Author's Bias)* **I**
While the passage is about fostering both cats and dogs, the author spends much more time talking about cats. We can *infer* that this is the author's preference.

Incorrect Answers:

A. The passage does not mention horses.

C. The author writes less about dogs than cats.

D. Puppies and kittens are not mentioned in the passage at all.

25. Correct Answer: B *(Making Inferences)*
The passage states that patience, time, and a little extra money are the qualities a person must have to be a good foster parent for an animal. You can deduce that it's more likely that a retired person has all three of these attributes.

Incorrect Answers:

A. Typically, teenagers don't have very much money, time, or patience, so they would not be good foster parents.

C. Time is stated as a requirement for being a good foster parent, so busy parents can be disqualified.

D. A person who travels a lot for work may have the money, but they would not be around enough to be a good foster parent.

Explanations for Test A Answers *(cont.)*

The King's Threads *(pages 28–33)*

26. Correct Answer: D *(Identifying Genre)*

This is a fairy tale as it is a far-fetched work of fiction featuring folklore characters like kings, villagers, and weavers.

Incorrect Answers:

A. The story is fiction, but it is a specific kind of fiction.

B. The story is not likely to happen in reality and contains no factual information.

C. Myths usually contain gods and explain the origin of natural events like the seasons.

27. Correct Answer: B *(Character Analysis, Traits)* **I**

The king is vain because he loves to dress up in fancy clothes and show himself off.

Incorrect Answers:

A. There is no one in the story that the king envies.

C. There is no evidence in the story to suggest that the king is very smart.

D. The king is not evil or wicked; he's just conceited.

28. Correct Answer: D *(Locating Details)* **E**

The story explicitly states that a single suit costs $100,000.

Incorrect Answers:

A. Five suits would cost $500,000.

B. The suit does not cost $50,000.

C. The suit does not cost $10,000.

29. Correct Answer: A *(Making Inferences)*

The designers know that there really isn't a suit and that the ministers are pretending that they see it.

Incorrect Answers:

B. While the designers do tell corny jokes, this is not what is making them laugh in this instance.

C. The ministers were not naked.

D. The ministers were not tickling the designers.

30. Correct Answer: A *(Making Inferences)* **I**

The king knows that he risks being exposed as a dishonest fool, so he sends his brightest and most truthful minister, because he believes that he will definitely be able to see the suit.

Incorrect Answers:

B. The king's motivation is fear, not authority.

C. The king is fearful but not of the designers.

D. The minister does not ask to go.

31. Correct Answer: D *(Identifying Figurative Language)*

"Holy Toledo" is an idiom, or a popular expression that is not taken literally.

Incorrect Answers:

A. A simile compares two things using *as* or *like*.

B. A metaphor is figurative language that also makes a comparison.

C. An *anagram* is a word that is scrambled to make another word.

32. Correct Answer: D *(Making inferences)* **I**

The text does not state explicitly why no one can really see the suit. It is implied that there really is not a suit.

Incorrect Answers:

A. There is no suit, so it can't be invisible.

B. The townspeople are liars and fools, but that is not why they can't see the suit.

C. There is no evidence to suggest that the townspeople are honest and smart.

33. Correct Answer: B *(Explicit, Recalling Details)*

The story states that the designers told everyone they met that they had a fabric that was invisible to anyone who was dishonest or stupid.

Incorrect Answers:

A. This is the opposite of what the story states.

C. The story does not make any connection to how you feel about the king and whether you could see or not see the suit.

D. The story does not say anything about not wanting to hurt the feelings of the king.

34. Correct Answer: A *(Making Inferences)*

The designers counted on no one being willing to admit to not seeing the suit for fear of their reputation.

Incorrect Answers:

B. People did not want to disagree with the ruler.

C. The suit was not magical. There was no suit.

D. The king did not issue any threat to his people. He did not make them pretend to see the suit.

35. Correct Answer: B *(Recalling Details)* **E**

During the parade, as the king strolls down the street, the boy yells, "Dad! Hey, Dad! Look at the king! He's naked!"

Incorrect Answers:

A. The boy's father pretends to see the suit and tries to silence his son.

C. Neither of the designers are at the parade.

D. The ministers who accompany the king go along with the charade.

Explanations for Test A Answers _(cont.)

The King's Threads (pages 28–33) *(cont.)*

36. Correct Answer: A *(Character Analysis)*

The adults are not his peers. There are no consequences for the boy speaking the truth.

Incorrect Answers:

B. There is no evidence that the boy is not bright.

C. The boy's father tries to get him to be quiet.

D. There is no evidence that the boy is the son of the king. The story refers to a man viewing the parade as the boy's father.

37. Correct Answer: D *(Making Inferences)*

The designers know that they have gotten away with an elaborate con (hoax) and don't want to get caught.

Incorrect Answers:

A. They are running for a train, not playing cards.

B. They are not making suits.

C. They are not sleeping.

38. Correct Answer: D *(Identifying Theme)*

All of the people in the town, with the exception of the little boy, pretend to see the king's suit even though there is no suit. If you go along with the group, and the group is wrong, it makes you look like a fool, too.

Incorrect Answers:

A. The king is vain, but he is not the only one who looks foolish.

B. Honesty is only one component of the theme of the story.

C. The con men do succeed, but only because the people were willing to go along with them.

Explanations for Test A Answers *(cont.)*

Frogs and Toads *(pages 34–38)*

39. Correct Answer: B *(Determining Meaning)*

Frogs can live in two different environments: on the land and in the water.

Incorrect Answers:

A. There is no mention of frog mating in the passage.

C. The passage doesn't say anything about frogs being twins.

D. The life span of the frog is not discussed.

40. Correct Answer: A *(Locating Details)* E

The passage states that there are over 4,000 different species of frogs.

Incorrect Answers:

B. The passage does not say there are 40,000 types of frogs.

C. The passage mentions the number 50, but does not say there are 50 types of frogs.

D. The passage does state how many different frog species there are.

41. Correct Answer: C *(Determining Meaning)*

The skin of the frog discharges a poison that is collected by native people and used on arrows.

Incorrect Answers:

A. The poison is released through the skin, not created there.

B. The poison is not hidden on the skin.

D. Nothing is combined or added to the poison.

42. Correct Answer: D *(Drawing Conclusions)* I

Nocturnal animals are active at night. You can deduce that during the day, they are resting or sleeping.

Incorrect Answers:

A. Nocturnal animals hunt at night.

B. Nocturnal animals spawn at night.

C. Nocturnal animals eat at night.

43. Correct Answer: B *(Determining Meaning)*

If many people enjoy eating frog's legs, then they must be very tasty.

Incorrect Answers:

A. They may be high in calories, but the passage does not suggest that this is why people like to eat them.

C. Foods that are popular are usually not bland.

D. A delicacy is usually expensive.

44. Correct Answer: A *(Making Inferences)* I

Webbed feet are an adaptation that help many animals swim in water.

Incorrect Answers:

B. The frog's sticky tongue help it catch flies, not their webbed feet.

C. Webbed feet have nothing to do with spawning.

D. A frog's strong back legs help it to jump.

45. Correct Answer: C *(Distinguishing Fact from Opinion)*

Even though the frog is an excellent jumper, this doesn't mean that it is better than other animals. You can't prove that a frog is superior to any other animal, only that it is a good jumper.

Incorrect Answers:

A. Frogs are good jumpers. This statement is a fact.

B. There are other animals that can jump as well as a frog. This statement is a fact.

D. Agreement does not determine if a statement is a fact or an opinion.

46. Correct Answer: B *(Determining Meaning, Context Clues)*

The sentence states that a toad can spend most of its life on the ground.

Incorrect Answers:

A. *Nocturnal* is not mentioned.

C. Ponds are not mentioned.

D. Insects are not mentioned.

47. Correct Answer: D *(Drawing Conclusions)*

The bulleted list states that toads do not have teeth, so you can deduce that frogs do.

Incorrect Answers:

A. The bulleted list states that toads do not have teeth.

B. Frogs can be many different colors, not just green.

C. Frogs and toads both begin as tadpoles.

48. Correct Answer: B *(Interpreting Graphic Features: Diagram)* E

The diagram shows that frogs form hind legs at eight weeks of age.

Incorrect Answers:

A. The passage does not say when the eggs hatch.

C. The tail shrinks after the frog is 12 weeks old.

D. The external gills disappear at six weeks.

49. Correct Answer: A *(Interpreting Graphic Features: Diagram)*

The diagram illustrates and states that tadpoles breathe through gills.

Incorrect Answers:

B. Fully-grown frogs have fully-formed lungs. A tadpole's lungs are not fully formed.

C. Tadpoles don't have fins.

D. *Frungs* is an invented word.

50. Correct Answer: B *(Drawing Conclusions)* I

You can deduce that both lungs for breathing oxygen and front legs for moving over the land are necessary for the frog to survive.

Incorrect Answers:

A. Frogs and tadpoles have smooth skin.

C. Tadpoles have hind legs.

D. Frogs and tadpoles have either gills or lungs, but not both at the same time.

Test B Answer Key

1. B	6. C	11. D	16. B	21. B	26. D	31. D	36. B	41. D	46. D
2. C	7. A	12. A	17. C	22. B	27. C	32. B	37. A	42. A	47. B
3. D	8. C	13. D	18. B	23. C	28. A	33. B	38. C	43. D	48. B
4. A	9. D	14. C	19. D	24. B	29. A	34. A	39. B	44. C	49. A
5. D	10. A	15. B	20. A	25. A	30. B	35. D	40. B	45. B	50. A

Explanations for Test B Answers

The Maya (pages 39–44)

1. **Correct Answer: B** (Author's Tone) **I**
   The author initiates a guessing game with readers. Games are associated with fun.
   Incorrect Answers:
   A. Guessing games are usually not serious.
   C. Guessing games are not usually sad.
   D. Sometimes guessing games can be confusing, but that is not their main purpose.

2. **Correct Answer: C** (Determining Meaning)
   The prefix *meso* means "in the middle." Central America is in the middle of North and South America.
   Incorrect Answers:
   A. Central America is one of the Americas, but this is not why it is called Mesoamerica.
   B. *Meso* does not mean "central."
   D. Central America is not located in the center of North America.

3. **Correct Answer: D** (Interpreting Graphic Features: Maps) **E**
   The map shows which locations are archaeological sites, meaning that they were once Maya cities, and also shows which sites are contemporary cities. Chiapas is not shown.
   Incorrect Answers:
   A. Tikal was a Maya city.
   B. Copan was a Maya city.
   D. Sayil was a Maya city.

4. **Correct Answer: A** (Drawing Conclusions) **I**
   The Maya ball game involves shooting a ball through a hoop, which can be best compared to basketball.
   Incorrect Answers:
   B. There are no bats in the Maya game.
   C. There are not nets or racquets in the Maya game.
   D. There are no sticks or pucks in the Maya game.

5. **Correct Answer: D** (Making Inferences)
   The Maya deliberately weakened their opponents to have a better chance of winning.
   Incorrect Answers:
   A. There is no direct mention of cheating.
   B. The king does not decide the winner.
   C. Play did not end when someone got hurt.

6. **Correct Answer: C** (Locating Details)
   The passage states that the Maya used the pyramids for religious ceremonies.
   Incorrect Answers:
   A. The Maya did use the pyramids as tombs, but not as a place to play ball games.
   B. The Maya did use the pyramids for worship, but not as a place to play ball games.
   D. Stargazing is not mentioned in the passage at all.

7. **Correct Answer: A** (Determining Meaning)
   The passage says the archaeologists uncover the pyramids. This implies that the pyramids were buried and had to be dug up. The prefix *ex* means "out of." In this case, digging the pyramid out of the earth.
   Incorrect Answers:
   B. Archaeologists had to uncover the pyramids, not cover them.
   C. *Excavate* means to "dig up" not "to study."
   D. The pyramids are not being rebuilt.

8. **Correct Answer: C** (Locating Details) **E**
   The passage states that *the calendar round* combines two other Maya calendars.
   Incorrect Answers:
   A. There is no mention of a sundial.
   B. There is a Maya calendar with 260 days, but it is not called the calendar round.
   D. There is a Maya calendar with 365 days, but it is not called the calendar round.

Explanations for Test B Answers (cont.)

The Maya (pages 39–44) (cont.)

9. **Correct Answer: D** (Distinguishing Fact from Opinion)
   A belief, even if held by many people, is an opinion because it cannot be proved using empirical evidence.
   Incorrect Answers:
   A. This is a fact.
   B. This is a statement.
   C. This is a fact.

10. **Correct Answer: A** (Locating Details)
   The list of ingredients does not include cream.
   Incorrect Answers:
   B. Milk is listed as an ingredient.
   C. Nutmeg is listed as an ingredient.
   D. Vanilla extract is listed as an ingredient.

11. **Correct Answer: D** (Determining Meaning)
   An *option* is something that you can decide whether you want to use or not. It is not a requirement.
   Incorrect Answers:
   A. *Necessary* is the opposite of *optional*.
   B. Cornstarch is the last item on the ingredient list, but "being last" is not the meaning of *optional*.
   C. *Optional* does not mean "expensive."

Lewis and Clarke Practice Math (pages 45–51)

12. **Correct Answer: A** (Locating Details)
   The passage states that Patrick is a fifth-grader at Franklin Middle School.
   Incorrect Answers:
   B. The story is not set in Patrick's bedroom.
   C. Hogwarts is where the Harry Potter books are set.
   D. The library is one specific setting of the larger story.

13. **Correct Answer: D** (Interpreting Figurative Language)
   Hyperbole is an exaggerated form of language. To say that a teacher is the hardest in the world or that you are imprisoned in a math class is an exaggeration of reality.
   Incorrect Answers:
   A. This is a realistic description of Patrick's situation.
   B. This sentence contains two idioms.
   C. This sentence contains a simile.

14. **Correct Answer: C** (Making Inferences) I
   The passage states that Patrick was staring out of the window wishing that he were riding his bike. He was not paying attention to his teacher.
   Incorrect Answers:
   A. Patrick was not sleeping in class.
   B. Patrick was not talking to a classmate during class.
   D. Patrick did not know the answer to the question and was not trying to work it out.

15. **Correct Answer: B** (Character Analysis) I
   Brandon's behavior shows that he was eager to tell Mr. Bone the right answer and eager to make Patrick feel bad about not knowing the answer.
   Incorrect Answers:
   A. Brandon does not act like a shy person. He draws attention to himself.
   C. Brandon doesn't act as if he is afraid. He gives Patrick a smug look.
   D. This can be disregarded because the options do provide the correct answer to the question.

16. **Correct Answer: B** (Interpreting Figurative Language)
   The phrase "hand shot up in the air like a sail on a windy day" is a simile as it compares two things using the word *like*.
   Incorrect Answers:
   A. This sentence is descriptive but does not contain a simile.
   C. This is an example of hyperbole.
   D. This is simply a declarative sentence.

17. **Correct Answer: C** (Identifying Literary Elements: Plot/Problem)
   The problem in the story is that Patrick is not good at math and is in danger of failing the class unless he passes a test for which he is unprepared.
   Incorrect Answers:
   A. The fact that Patrick reads lots of Harry Potter books is not a problem for him.
   B. Barry does like to eat gummy bears, but this is not a problem that pertains to the plot of the story.
   D. Mr. Bone called on Patrick in class, but that doesn't mean he is picking on him.

18. **Correct Answer: B** (Determining Meaning)
   The paragraph states that Patrick reads all of the time, so we can deduce that he loves to read.
   Incorrect Answers:
   A. A slow and plodding reader probably does not like to read often, as it would be difficult.
   C. Professor Lewis says that his son reads all of the time, not occasionally.
   D. There is no evidence to suggest that *voracious* has something to do with reading in the dark.

19. **Correct Answer: D** (Interpreting Figurative Language)
   The phrase "it would be curtains" is an idiom meaning that something would be disastrous.
   Incorrect Answers:
   A. A *metaphor* compares two thing without using the words *like* or *as*.
   B. *Onomatopoeia* is a word that sounds like what it is describing.
   C. An *analogy* is a comparison of two similar objects.

Explanations for Test B Answers *(cont.)*

Lewis and Clarke Practice Math *(pages 45–51)* *(cont.)*

20. Correct Answer: A *(Making Inferences)* **I**

Mr. Bone and Professor Lewis are making math problems out of how fast Patrick can read, and math is the very thing that Patrick has trouble understanding.

Incorrect Answers:

B. They are adults, but this is not why Patrick is confused by their conversation.

C. Patrick does daydream, but he is not daydreaming in this instance.

D. Patrick does not have his fingers in his ears.

21. Correct Answer: B *(Making Deductions)*

Lewis and Clark were a famous team; Patrick and Barry feel that they are also a team.

Incorrect Answers:

A. They do know each other's first names.

C. It is not a rule of Franklin Middle School.

D. Obviously, they know each other.

22. Correct Answer: B *(Making Deductions)*

Patrick and Barry's friendship is based on a mutual love of Harry Potter books.

Incorrect Answers:

A. Patrick is not great at math. That's why Barry is helping him.

C. The story doesn't say that they are both in Mr. Bone's class.

D. Only Barry loves gummy bears.

An Emerald Is as Green as Grass *(pages 52–53)*

23. Correct Answer: C *(Interpreting Figurative Language: Simile)*

The first three lines of the poem are similes. Similes usually use the words *as* or *like* to compare things.

Incorrect Answers:

A. There are no examples of hyperbole in the poem at all.

B. There are no examples of personification in the poem at all.

D. There are no examples of alliteration in the poem at all.

24. Correct Answer: B *(Interpreting Poetry: Rhyme Scheme)*

The second and fourth lines of each stanza rhyme. The first and third do not.

Incorrect Answers:

A. The rhyme scheme aabb means that lines 1 and 2 rhyme, and lines 3 and 4 rhyme.

C. The rhyme scheme abcd would mean that there are no lines that rhyme.

D. The form baba is not a rhyme scheme.

25. Correct Answer: A *(Locating Details)* **E**

The first stanza says that the flint can be found in the mud.

Incorrect Answers:

B. The second stanza does not say where the flint can be found.

C. The location of the flint is only mentioned in the first stanza.

D. The location of the flint is mentioned in the last line of the first stanza.

26. Correct Answer: D *(Interpreting Poetry)*

The poem says that the world desires the diamond.

Incorrect Answers:

A. The flint may be useful, but it is not desired.

B. The opal is like a rainbow, but it is not desired.

C. The ruby is beautiful, but not as desired as the diamond.

27. Correct Answer: C *(Interpreting Poetry)*

The poem says "An opal holds a fiery spark." Glitter is sparkly.

Incorrect Answers:

A. A sapphire is blue.

B. A diamond is described as brilliant.

D. An emerald is green.

28. Correct Answer: A *(Interpreting Poetry: Author's Point of View)* **I**

The poem says that a flint *holds* fire, meaning that with it you can make fire, which is useful.

Incorrect Answers:

B. The poet only describes how a diamond looks, not how useful it is.

C. The poet only describes how beautiful a sapphire is, not how useful it may be.

D. The poet writes about many stones but singles out the flint and describes its use, not how it looks.

29. Correct Answer: A *(Interpreting Poetry)*

Flint stones hold fire because they can be hit against one another to create sparks, which can then light a fire.

Incorrect Answers:

B. A flint stone is not bright, but rather dark.

C. A flint stone feels the same temperature as any other rock or mineral.

D. A flint stone can make fire, but it is not made from fire.

30. Correct Answer: B *(Interpreting Poetry: Theme)*

The flint is the only stone that has a practical use in the real world. It can make fire. Its practicality is what makes it precious or valuable.

Incorrect Answers:

A. Beautiful stones are not practical and therefore not as valuable.

C. Shiny stones may be the most beautiful, but *value*, not beauty, is the theme of the poem.

D. The flint is beautiful because it is practical.

Explanations for Test B Answers *(cont.)*

The Jobs of Steve Jobs *(pages 54–56)*

31. Correct Answer: D *(Locating Details)* **E**

The author compares Steve Jobs to Thomas Edison and Henry Ford.

Incorrect Answers:

A. Franklin is not mentioned.

B. Bell is not mentioned.

C. Carver is not mentioned.

32. Correct Answer: B *(Making Inferences)* **I**

The electric light would provide light during day and night. Light is a requirement for reading.

Incorrect Answers:

A. You don't need light to sleep.

C. You can tell stories in the dark.

D. You don't need light to feed your horse.

33. Correct Answer: B *(Making Deductions)*

Many people have nicknames that are abbreviations of their names. "Woz" is a shortened version of Wozniak.

Incorrect Answers:

A. Woz is not the Apple II.

C. Woz Is not the Apple I.

D. Steve Jobs is not called Woz.

34. Correct Answer: A *(Locating Details)* **E**

The passage clearly states that Steve Jobs and Steve Wozniak made the Atari circuit board smaller.

Incorrect Answers:

B. The circuit board was simplified, not made more complex.

C. The military is mentioned in the passage but not in reference to the Atari circuit board.

D. They did not invent the first computer game.

35. Correct Answer: D *(Locating Details)*

Ford made the automobile more affordable for regular people, and Jobs made the personal computer more affordable for the average American.

Incorrect Answers:

A. There is no mention of Ford's experience in college.

B. They probably both do have patents, but the passage does not discuss this.

C. They are both American, but the passage does not refer to this.

36. Correct Answer: B *(Locating Details)*

Steve Jobs admired the Beatles and named his company after theirs.

Incorrect Answers:

A. Steve Jobs is not related to any of the Beatles.

C. The Beatles did not write a song about Jobs.

D. iTunes does sell Beatles songs, but this is not the strongest connection between them.

37. Correct Answer: A *(Locating Details)*

The passage clearly states that the Apple II was the name of the first personal computer.

Incorrect Answers:

B. The passage does not mention the Apple I.

C. Atari is the name of the game company where Steve Jobs worked.

D. Hewlett-Packard is the name of a company where Jobs worked after he left college.

38. Correct Answer: C *(Making Inferences)*

People did not search the Internet on the Apple II. The Internet hadn't been invented yet.

Incorrect Answers:

A. The passage makes no mention of the Apple I.

B. The Internet as we know it was unavailable at that time. People used books, magazines, etc., at the library for research, not the Internet.

D. There were no iPhones at that time.

Explanations for Test B Answers *(cont.)*

Hawk Mountain (pages 57–61)

39. Correct Answer: B *(Locating Details)* **E**

The passage clearly states that Hawk Mountain is located in Pennsylvania.

Incorrect Answers:

A. There is no mention of Virginia.

C. This is an invented location.

D. There is no mention of New York.

40. Correct Answer: B (Determining Meaning)

The passage states that a refuge is a place that protects the health and safety of certain types of animals. It says that Mrs. Edge created a sanctuary at Hawk Mountain to protect the birds from being hunted.

Incorrect Answers:

A. A zoo keeps animals safe, but that is not its main purpose.

C. A park may have animals in it, but its mission is not to protect them.

D. A hospital takes care of sick people and animals.

41. Correct Answer: D *(Making Deductions)* **I**

Birds of prey hunt live, small animals. A chipmunk is a small mammal.

Incorrect Answers:

A. A horse would be too large an animal for a bird to hunt, kill, and eat.

B. Birds of prey eat mostly mammals.

C. Birds of prey are carnivores, not herbivores.

42. Correct Answer: A *(Making Inferences)* **I**

The passage states that the niche of the birds of prey is to keep the population of small animals in check. You can deduce that if the birds were gone, the population would grow because they would not be subject to predation.

Incorrect Answers:

B. Small rodents would not be hunted as much. Their population would get larger, not smaller.

C. The vegetation on the mountain is not directly affected by birds of prey.

D. Hunters are no longer paid to kill birds of prey at Hawk Mountain.

43. Correct Answer: D (Interpreting Figurative Language)

"Caught eye" is an idiom that is not meant to be taken literally.

Incorrect Answers:

A. "Caught the eye" does not mean to get poked in the eye.

B. "Caught the eye" does not mean to take a photograph.

C. "Caught the eye" does not mean to be a conservationist.

44. Correct Answer: C *(Making Deductions)*

The passage states that Mrs. Edge installed a warden at Hawk Mountain to prevent hunters from killing the birds. The warden enforces the law.

Incorrect Answers:

A. The warden is not reporting on the events at Hawk Mountain.

B. School principals generally enforce rules, not laws.

D. Veterinarians are animal doctors.

45. Correct Answer: B *(Interpreting Graphic Features: Table)* **E**

The table clearly states that there were 21 sharp–shinned hawks on October 15th.

Incorrect Answers:

A. There were two black vultures on October 15th.

C. There were no rough-legged hawks sighted on October 15th.

D. This is not a quantity stated on the table.

46. Correct Answer: D *(Interpreting Graphic Features: Table)*

The table clearly states that the highest daily count for red–tailed hawks is 62.

Incorrect Answers:

A. 266 is the amount of sharp–shinned hawks for this category.

B. 6 is the amount of black vultures for this category.

C. This is not a quantity stated for this category.

47. Correct Answer: B *(Locating Details)* **E**

The passage states that the blaze marks are there to keep you from getting lost.

Incorrect Answers:

A. The blaze marks give no indication about the level of difficulty of the trail.

C. The blaze marks have nothing to do with viewing the birds.

D. The blaze marks do not prevent fires of any kind.

48. Correct Answer: B *(Making Inferences)* **I**

It is a short hike that may be more appropriate for both the young and the old.

Incorrect Answers:

A. The Lookout Trail is an easy hike.

C. There is no mention of benches in the passage.

D. It does have fantastic views, but so do the other trails mentioned.

49. Correct Answer: A *(Locating Details)*

The Golden Eagle Trail requires the hiker to climb up 800 feet.

Incorrect Answers:

B. Climbing down is not as difficult as climbing up.

C. You don't climb over the ridge of the mountain on this hike.

D. The elevation on this trail is not 1,500 feet.

50. Correct Answer: A *(Locating Details)*

The passage states that the Skyline Trail connects to the Appalachian Trail.

Incorrect Answers:

B. The Golden Eagle Trail doesn't connect to the Appalachian Trail.

C. There is no Blaze Trail.

D. The River of Rocks Trail doesn't connect to the Appalachian Trail.

Test C Answer Key

1. D	6. D	11. A	16. B	21. B	26. C	31. D	36. D	41. B	46. A
2. C	7. A	12. D	17. A	22. C	27. A	32. A	37. A	42. D	47. D
3. B	8. C	13. C	18. D	23. D	28. D	33. C	38. B	43. B	48. A
4. B	9. A	14. D	19. D	24. A	29. A	34. B	39. D	44. A	49. C
5. C	10. C	15. D	20. A	25. D	30. B	35. C	40. A	45. B	50. C

Explanations for Test C Answers

The Land of Nod (pages 62–64)

1. **Correct Answer: D** (Interpreting Poetry)
   The poem has four stanzas.
   Incorrect Answers:
   A. The poem does not have 1 stanza.
   B. The poem does not have 2 stanzas.
   C. The poem has 16 lines, but not 16 stanzas.

2. **Correct Answer: C** (Interpreting Poetry)
   Dreams are generated in a person's mind, so the land of Nod is in a person's head.
   Incorrect Answers:
   A. The land of Nod is not located in another country.
   B. The land of Nod is not located in another town.
   D. The narrator specifically says "go abroad," but that is not where the land of Nod is located.

3. **Correct Answer: B** (Interpreting Poetry: Rhyme Scheme)
   The first and second lines rhyme and the third and fourth lines of each stanza rhyme.
   Incorrect Answers:
   A. This rhyme scheme would mean that the first and third, and the second and fourth lines in each stanza rhyme.
   C. This would mean that no lines rhyme.
   D. This is not a rhyme scheme.

4. **Correct Answer: B** (Interpreting Poetry)
   The narrator is speaking about his dreams as if they were another physical place.
   Incorrect Answers:
   A. There is no mention of a hospital in the poem.
   C. The narrator is probably dreaming in his bedroom, but this is not the place he is describing.
   D. The narrator does describe his dreams as strange and foreign, but he only means this figuratively, not literally.

5. **Correct Answer: C** (Interpreting Poetry)
   The narrator is dreaming, not physically traveling anywhere. You can dream about people, but you can't intentionally take them with you into your own dreams.
   Incorrect Answers:
   A. The narrator actually implies that he wishes he could take someone with him to tell him what to do.
   B. The poem does not say anything about anyone not wanting to go with him.
   D. There is no mention of any rules regarding the land of Nod.

6. **Correct Answer: D** (Interpreting Poetry)
   The narrator states in the third stanza, "The strangest things are there for me."
   Incorrect Answers:
   A. The narrator does not say that the land of Nod is exciting.
   B. The narrator is definitely not bored in the land of Nod.
   C. There is no mention of the temperature in the land of Nod.

7. **Correct Answer: A** (Interpreting Poetry)
   Nearly all people stop dreaming when they wake.
   Incorrect Answers:
   B. No train or boat is required because the narrator is not physically traveling anywhere.
   C. The narrator does not walk out of the land of Nod, as it is his dreams.
   D. The narrator does speak about the mountainsides of dreams, but it has nothing to do with returning from the land of Nod.

8. **Correct Answer: C** (Interpreting Poetry)
   The land of Nod is the land of dreams. The only way to get there is to fall asleep, which most people usually do at night, not during the day.
   Incorrect Answers:
   A. There is no mention of the narrator's parents.
   B. Streams are mentioned in the poem, but it has nothing to do with getting back and forth from the land of Nod.
   D. The narrator does mention music, but it has nothing to do with getting to and from the land of Nod.

Explanations for Test C Answers *(cont.)*

The Land of Nod *(pages 62–64) (cont.)*

9. **Correct Answer: A** *(Interpreting Poetry)*

   The narrator is saying that even though he tries to remember the strange and curious things he saw and heard in his dreams, he can't quite recall them. Once you wake up from a dream, it is often hard to remember all of the details.

   Incorrect Answers:
   B. Having a poor memory is not the reason the narrator can't remember his dreams.
   C. The narrator may be confused about what he dreams, but this is not the reason he can't remember them.
   D. The narrator describes the music as "curious" but doesn't say that he dislikes it.

10. **Correct Answer: C** *(Interpreting Poetry)*

    The feeling or tone of the poem is haunting. The narrator is haunted by dreams that he can't quite remember.

    Incorrect Answers:
    A. The poem does not have a funny tone.
    B. While the narrator may have some strange experiences in his dreams, he wants to return.
    D. The poem is not sarcastic, but instead is very earnest.

How to Make Compost *(pages 65–67)*

11. **Correct Answer: A** *(Locating Details)*

    In the first paragraph, it clearly states that photosynthesis is the process used by plants to make food.

    Incorrect Answers:
    B. Plants do not make compost.
    C. Plants do not produce nutrients that they feed on.
    D. Osmosis describes a process not relevant in this context.

12. **Correct Answer: D** *(Making Deductions)*

    Organic matter was once alive. Pens are made from synthetic materials that have never been alive.

    Incorrect Answers:
    A. A banana is an example of organic material because it is alive.
    B. A spider is an example of organic material because it is alive.
    C. A leather purse is an example of organic material because it is made from something that was once alive.

13. **Correct Answer: C** *(Locating Details)*

    The passage clearly states in the third paragraph that the two basic elements of compost are nitrogen and carbon.

    Incorrect Answers:
    A. Carbon is mentioned as one of the ingredients but not oxygen.
    B. Hydrogen is not mentioned as an essential ingredient of compost.
    D. Nitrogen is mentioned, but the question asks for two ingredients, not one.

14. **Correct Answer: D** *(Making Deductions)*

    Compost needs to be in an elevated, dry, and sunny spot. None of the options states this.

    Incorrect Answers:
    A. Compost needs sun, not shade.
    B. Compost needs to be moist, not soaked.
    C. Compost needs to be in an elevated area, not in a ditch.

15. **Correct Answer: D** *(Locating Details)*

    In the directions, Step 2 states that the first layer of compost is made of dried leaves, grass clippings, and twigs.

    Incorrect Answers:
    A. Eggshells and coffee grounds may be used but not as a first layer.
    B. Shredded newspapers may be used but not as a first layer.
    C. Weed killer is not mentioned as something that should be used in compost.

16. **Correct Answer: B** *(Making Inferences)*

    The passage states that dairy products should not be used in compost. Cheese is a dairy product.

    Incorrect Answers:
    A. You may use eggshells in compost.
    C. Fruit peels may be used in compost.
    D. Straw may be used in compost.

17. **Correct Answer: A** *(Locating Details)*

    In the directions, Step 7 states that the compost should be mixed up weekly.

    Incorrect Answers:
    B. Water may be added, but on an "as needed" basis, not weekly.
    C. The passage does not suggest taking the bag off weekly.
    D. The passage does not instruct to add weed killer to the compost.

18. **Correct Answer: D** *(Making Deductions)*

    Organic matter is material that was once living. Paper comes from trees that were once alive; therefore, paper is considered organic.

    Incorrect Answers:
    A. This is the opposite of what organic material is.
    B. Paper is recyclable, but that is not why it is considered organic.
    C. Paper should be shredded before it is added to the compost, but that is not what makes it organic.

Explanations for Test C Answers *(cont.)*

How to Make Compost *(pages 65–67)* *(cont.)*

19. Correct Answer: D *(Locating Details)*

Step 6 of the directions states that the compost should be kept moist.

Incorrect Answers:

A. The compost should not be in a dry place. It should be moist.

B. There is a difference between moist (wetness) and cool (temperature).

C. The passage states that compost should be kept in a sunny spot.

20. Correct Answer: A *(Making Inferences)*

The organic material that is used in composting (newspapers, coffee grounds, eggshells) would be thrown in the trash. By reusing them, we are creating fewer waste products to be recycled in factories.

Incorrect Answers:

B. Compost does not require the use of chemicals, but that is not the reason it reduces waste.

C. A compost pile does take up space.

D. Compost is organic, but this is not why it reduces waste.

Sam the Magnificent *(pages 68–70)*

21. Correct Answer: B *(Identifying Main Character)*

Sam is the main character of the story as all of the events revolve around him.

Incorrect Answers:

A. Houdini is a famous magician who Sam read about, but he is not the main character.

C. Sam performs a magic trick on his father, but his father is not the main character. Sam's father is not even named in the story.

D. Sam performs a magic trick on his mother, but she is not the main character. Sam's mother is not even named in the story.

22. Correct Answer: C *(Recalling Details)*

Houdini is a famous magician about whom Sam read a biography.

Incorrect Answers:

A. Houdini is not a teacher. The story does not mention any teachers.

B. Houdini is not Sam's father.

D. Houdini is not a former senator. The story does not mention any senators.

23. Correct Answer: D *(Recalling Details)*

The story says that Houdini was a famous escape artist and talks about his famous Milk Can Escape.

Incorrect Answers:

A. The story mentions that Sam learned card tricks but not that Houdini did.

B. The story mentions that Sam learned how to do some tricks with coins but not that Houdini did.

C. The story says nothing about Houdini being famous for great feats of strength.

24. Correct Answer: A *(Character Analysis, Motivation)*

After reading a biography about Houdini, Sam is inspired, or motivated, to learn how to be a magician. Usually when people copy the actions of others, it means that they admire them in some way.

Incorrect Answers:

B. There is nothing to suggest in the story that Sam is afraid of Houdini. Remember, Sam does not know Houdini.

C. There is nothing to suggest that Sam is annoyed by Houdini. For Sam, Houdini is a historical figure. It is hard to get annoyed by someone who no longer exists.

D. There is nothing to suggest that Sam is jealous of Houdini. Sometimes a jealous person will copy the actions of the person of whom he or she is jealous, but it is usually accompanied by boasting or meanness.

25. Correct Answer: D *(Recalling Details)*

The story tells that Sam names his famous trick *Pick a Number*.

Incorrect Answers:

A. The Milk Can Escape is the name of one of Houdini's famous tricks.

B. The story does not mention a trick called the Handcuff Escape.

C. The story does not mention a trick called the Houdini Classic.

26. Correct Answer: C *(Recalling Details)*

The story says that during the Milk Can Escape, Houdini's hands and feet would be handcuffed and he would be sealed and locked in a large milk can.

Incorrect Answers:

A. The story says that Houdini did do escapes from wooden chests, but this is not the Milk Can Escape.

B. Houdini may have performed escapes in which he was handcuffed and locked in a wooden crate, but this is not the Milk Can Escape.

D. The Milk Can Escape does not involve making a milk can disappear.

Explanations for Test C Answers (cont.)

Sam the Magnificent (pages 68–70) (cont.)

27. Correct Answer: A (*Recalling Details*)

Sam's trick requires that you choose a number from one to five.

Incorrect Answers:

B. Three is not the correct answer.

C. Ten is not the correct answer.

D. Two is not the correct answer.

28. Correct Answer: D (*Sequence of Events*)

Sam performs the trick on his dad first.

Incorrect Answers:

A. The story does not mention a friend called Harry. Harry is Houdini's first name.

B. Sam performs the trick on his mother second.

C. There is no uncle in the story.

29. Correct Answer: A (*Making Inferences*)

The trick is set up so it makes it look as if the person performing it can read people's minds, or guess the number they are thinking of.

Incorrect Answers:

B. The person doing the trick has to hide paper, but finding paper or guessing where paper is hidden is not a part of the trick.

C. There are no rabbits or hats in the story.

D. The story talks about Houdini's amazing escapes, but this has nothing to do with the trick Sam does.

30. Correct Answer: B (*Making Deductions*)

You can deduce that magicians generally do not tell how they do their tricks. If they did, it would not appear magical.

Incorrect Answers:

A. There is nothing to suggest that Sam is angry with his parents. In fact, it looks as if he has a playful relationship with them.

C. Sam set up the trick, so you can assume that he would know how to explain it.

D. There is nothing to suggest that Sam is spoiled.

Sam's Pick a Number Trick (pages 71–74)

31. Correct Answer: D (*Determining Meaning*)

The passage states that a *prestidigitator* is a fancy word for a magician.

Incorrect Answers:

A. Some prestidigitators are also escape artists, but the word itself means magician.

B. The trickee is the person on whom the trick is being played.

C. There is no mention of a trickster in the story.

32. Correct Answer: A (*Making Deductions*)

The trick requires that a person pick a number from one to five.

Incorrect Answers:

B. Five is an odd number, but that has nothing to do with the trick.

C. There are five fingers on each hand, but this is inconsequential to the performance of the trick.

D. Five is half of ten, but this does not have anything to do with the trick.

33. Correct Answer: C (*Recalling Details*)

The instructions clearly state that "I knew you would pick 1, 2, 3, 4, or 5" would be written on the individual pieces of paper.

Incorrect Answers:

A. "I saw you!" would not be written on the paper.

B. "Gotcha!" would not be written on the paper.

D. "You can't fool me!" would not be written on the paper.

34. Correct Answer: B (*Determining Meaning*)

The passage states, in step 7, that the *trickee* is the person being tricked.

Incorrect Answers:

A. The trickee is not the person performing the trick.

C. The magician is the person performing the trick, not the person on whom the trick is being performed.

D. *Prestidigitator* is a synonym for *magician*, so this would not be the trickee.

35. Correct Answer: C (*Making Deductions*)

The trick is to create the illusion that the person performing it can guess the number the person is thinking. If the audience saw the magician hiding the paper, they would be able to guess how the illusion was created.

Incorrect Answers:

A. Part of the trick is that the pieces of paper are discovered by the trickee.

B. This has nothing to do with the trick.

D. You can't select "none of these" unless all of the options are incorrect.

Explanations for Test C Answers *(cont.)*

Sam's Pick a Number Trick *(pages 71–74) (cont.)*

36. Correct Answer: D *(Locating Details)*

Step 8 clearly states that you ask the trickee to pick a number from one to five.

Incorrect Answers:

A. "Wait for an opportunity when the trickee is in the room where you hid the papers" is Step 7.

B. Telling the trickee to look under the plant pot is not a step in the trick.

C. Hiding the paper is done in Step 5.

37. Correct Answer: A *(Making Deductions)*

Not only do the instructions alert the reader to the fact that remembering where the papers are hidden is important, you can deduce that not remembering where you hid them would completely ruin the trick. It would destroy the illusion that you could guess what the "trickee" was thinking.

Incorrect Answers:

B. Writing clearly may be important but it is not the most important part of the trick.

C. Selecting good hiding places is important, but probably not as important as remembering where the papers are hidden.

D. Explaining the trick to the trickee is not a part of the trick. The instructions say never to reveal your secrets.

38. Correct Answer: B *(Making Deductions)*

If you forget where you have hidden the papers, it will ruin the illusion that you can guess what number people are thinking.

Incorrect Answers:

A. Selecting bad hiding places may compromise the trick but not as much as forgetting where the papers are hidden.

C. The instructions don't mention any magic words that are needed to do the trick.

D. The trick might fail if the trickee figures it out, but forgetting where you hid the papers would be even more disastrous.

39. Correct Answer: D *(Making Deductions)*

It would be very difficult to remember the hiding places of more than five pieces of paper. Since the success of the trick is dependent upon the magician remembering where the papers are hidden, it is safer to keep it to five.

Incorrect Answers:

A. There is no mention of five being the lucky number of magicians.

B. The ability to do the trick with small children is not the reason the numbers are limited to five.

C. The trick would take the same amount of time, no matter how many numbers are involved.

40. Correct Answer: A *(Making Deductions)*

The trick requires some preparation, which the trickee cannot be permitted to see. Once the trick is performed, and a number is selected, you would need time to set up the trick again. You would be unable to do this if the trickee were still present.

Incorrect Answers:

B. Hiding a few pieces of paper would not be considered exhausting.

C. Usually, people do like to see tricks performed more than once, so they can try to figure them out.

D. You can never select "all of these" if one of the options is incorrect.

Explanations for Test C Answers (cont.)

Edible Insects! (pages 75–77)

41. Correct Answer: B (Determining Meaning, Context Clues)

The beginning of the passage talks about the fact that in some parts of the world people eat insects. You can infer then that *edible* means *eatable*.

Incorrect Answers:

A. *Edible* is not a synonym for *insect*.

C. Something that is not eaten by people would be the opposite of what *edible* means.

D. *Edible* does not mean *recipe*.

42. Correct Answer: D (Identifying Prefixes)

The passage states that the prefix *ento* means insect.

Incorrect Answers:

A. *Phagy* is the suffix.

B. *Mophagy* is not the prefix.

C. *En* is not the prefix. It is just the first two letters of the word.

43. Correct Answer: B (Locating Details)

Cicadas are the insects in the cookie recipe.

Incorrect Answers:

A. Chips are not the insects in the recipe.

C. Mealworms are mentioned in the passage, but they are not the insects in the cookie recipe.

D. Grasshoppers are mentioned in the passage, but they are not the insects in the cookie recipe.

44. Correct Answer: A (Locating Details)

The recipe calls for one teaspoon of salt.

Incorrect Answers:

B. The recipe does not call for three teaspoons of salt.

C. The recipe does not call for ¾ of a teaspoon of salt.

D. The recipe does not call for one tablespoon of salt.

45. Correct Answer: B (Making Deductions)

The butter has to be mixed with the other ingredients. It would be nearly impossible to stir in hard butter.

Incorrect Answers:

A. Softened butter tastes the same as hard butter.

C. There is no indication that softened butter works better with insect recipes.

D. The inclusion of softened butter has nothing to do with the author's preference. Many recipes call for softened butter because it is easier to mix.

46. Correct Answer: A (Locating Details)

The recipe states that ¾ of a cup of cicadas are required.

Incorrect Answers:

B. A handful is not required.

C. Ten are not required.

D. Three are not required.

47. Correct Answer: D (Steps in a Process)

The step directly before adding the eggs to the butter mixture is "In a small bowl, crack the eggs and beat them with a fork."

Incorrect Answers:

A. This step comes after you add the eggs to the butter mixture.

B. You don't stir in the chocolate chips and cicadas at this point.

C. Preheating the oven is the first thing you do.

48. Correct Answer: A (Making Deductions)

The recipe says to bake the cookies for 8–10 minutes. You can deduce that if you bake them longer, you run the risk of burning them.

Incorrect Answers:

B. Twelve minutes is longer than the recipe requires, so there is no chance they would be undercooked.

C. The cicadas are not alive before the cookies go into the oven.

D. The cookies are probably at their best when they have been baked between 8–10 minutes.

49. Correct Answer: C (Locating Details)

The recipe calls for roasted, salted cicadas.

Incorrect Answers:

A. There is no mention of sugar-coated cicadas.

B. There is no mention of live cicadas.

D. There is no mention of cicada larvae.

50. Correct Answer: C (Making Inferences)

Most people like to know and have control over what they put in their mouths. It is very likely that most people would be very annoyed to discover that they ate something without their knowledge that they probably would not have chosen to eat.

Incorrect Answers:

A. Silly implies an element of fun. Most Americans would not think eating insects is fun.

B. Some people might be sad, but this is not the best choice here given the other options.

D. People usually get bored when there is nothing going on or when they are doing something that they do all the time. Eating cicadas doesn't fit these two criteria.